RAINY DAYS & SATURDAYS

RAINY DAYS & SATURDAYS

By Linda Hetzer

Illustrated by Deborah Zemke

Workman Publishing, New York

Library of Congress Cataloging-in-Publication Data
Hetzer, Linda.
Rainy days & Saturdays / by Linda Hetzer.
p. cm.
Includes index.
ISBN 1-56305-513-9 (paper)
1. Indoor games. 2. Amusements. I. Title. II. Title: Rainy days and Saturdays.
GV1229.H48 1995
793'.01'922—dc20

Cover design by Paul Gamarello
Book design by Paul Gamarello with Gwen Petruska
Illustrations by Deborah Zemke

Workman books are available at special discount when purchased in bulk for special premiums and sales promotions as well as for fund-raising or educational use. Special editions or books excepts also can be created to specification. For details, contact the Special Sales Director at the address below.

Workman Publishing Company, Inc.
708 Broadway
New York, NY 10003-9555

Manufactured in the United States of America

First Printing January 1996
10 9 8 7 6 5 4 3 2 1

**TO EMILY AND ELIZABETH
WITH LOVE AND
THE HOPE OF MANY
MORE RAINY DAYS TOGETHER**

A book is always a collaboration of ideas, so I am grateful to all those who shared their knowledge, their skills, and their inspiration. Thanks to the people at Workman: Suzanne Rafer for her insight and Margot Herrera for her unfailing good cheer. A special thanks to Michael Ginsburg and to Emily and Elizabeth whose special talents and inexhaustible imaginations are a large part of this book.

CONTENTS

INTRODUCTION Getting Started..............X

1. BIG ADVENTURES 1
Open a Restaurant....................................2
Camp In 4
Have an Indoor Parade..............................6
Plan a Carnival 8
Produce a TV Show 10
Take a Cruise... Or Ride the Rails 12
Wake Up to an Opposite Morning 14
Quick Trick Have a Sing-Along 15
Put on a Puppet Show 16
Create an Artists' Studio 18
Build a Haunted Hallway 20

2. GAMES 23
Make Your Own Board Game 24
Connect Four...26
Botticelli Junior 27
Quick Trick Moody Blue 28
You Don't Know What You're Talking About ...29
Name That Number 30
Nim Skills 31
Two-Sided Puzzle 32

3. MYSTERIOUS FUN 33
Invisible Ink 34
Secret Code 35
Mystery Bags............ 36
Hide in Plain Sight........ 37
Pass It Along 38
Quick Trick Freaky Folds 38
Magazine Scavenger Hunt 39
Buried Treasure 40

4. STRING FLING 41
Friendship Bracelet 42
String Balloon 44
Macramé Key Chain 45
Quick Trick Brushless Painting 47
Straight Curves 48
Twined Yarn Basket 50
Yarn-Covered Vase 52
Yarn Belt...54
Miniature God's-Eye...................................56
Yarn Spiderweb 58

5. INDOOR SPORTS 59
Miniature Golf 60
Bowling 62
Balloon Volleyball 63
Wastebasket Ball 64
Quick Trick Cup Catch 64
Obstacle Course 65

Skee Ball 66
Quick Trick Sardines 66
A Day at the Races 67

6. SCIENTIFIC STUFF 69
Blow Your Stack.................................70
Hairy Harry 71
Periscope Up 72
Electromagnet 73
Kitchen Garden 74
Capture Your Shadow 76
Quick Trick Dollar Bridge 77
Feed the Birds 78
Quick Trick Bath Cents 79
Tabletop Terrarium 80
Rainwater Watching 81
Quick Trick Lasso an Ice Cube 82
Good Vibes 84

7. THE FAMILY HISTORIAN 85
Read All About It 86
A Day in the Life of Your Family 88
Relatively Trivial 89
Interview Your Grandparents 90
Special Event Album 92
A Bow Tie Wall Hanging 94
Frame Your Family 96
Grow a Family Tree...........................98
A Family Photo Album 100

8. NEAT TREATS 103
Kitchen Basics 104
French Bread Pizza 105
Quesadillas 106

Popovers 107
Tuna Faces 108
Quick Trick Homemade Soda 109
Yogurt Cheese 110
Zesty Toasted Cheese Sandwiches 111
Mixed Green Salad and Vinaigrette 112
Baked Apples 113
Fruit Kebabs 114
Orange Cream Pops 115
Frozen Bananas 116
Quick Trick Trail Mix 117
Chocolate Chip Muffins 118
Lemon Drop Cookies 120
Banana Smoothie 121
Chocolate Crunch Bars 122
Banana S'mores 124
Ice Cream Sandwiches 125
Gummy Raindrops 126

9. CREATIVE THINKING 127
Your Own Cartoon Strips 128
Create a Story 129
Write and Illustrate a Book 130
Haiku and Cinquain 132
Brainstorm 133
Keep a Journal 134
Be Pen Pal 136
Take a Trip to Mars... Back in History........138
Be an Interior Decorator....................139

10. READY TO WEAR 141

Special T 142
Personalized Lunch Bags 143
Money Pouch 144
Dough Monster Chain 146
Magazine Beads 147
Ponytail Holder 148
Quick Trick Ribbon-Covered Headband 149
Bow Barrette 150
Safety Pin Bracelet 151

11. MAGIC TRICKS 153

Tips From Mondo the Magnificent 154
Chained! 155
George Flips! 156
Vanna Vanishes 157
The Jacks Tell All 158
The Psychic 159
Column by Column 160
Knot? Not! 161
Loopy Loops 162
Quick Trick The Hidden Penny Trick 163
Banana Split 164
Keep It Dry 165
Quick Trick The Unpoppable Balloon 166

12. RAINY-DAY BANDSTAND 167

Glass Chimes 168
Kooky Kazoos 169
A Drum to Keep the Beat 170
Merry Maracas 172
Tinkly Tambourine 173
Rubber Band Guitar 174
Quick Trick You've Got Rhythm 175
Nailhead Xylophone 176

13. NUMBER FUN 177

Number One 178
Forever 37 179
Quick Trick Number Palindrome 179
Take It to the Nines 180
A Magic Number 181
The Sum of Them 182
Toothpick Tally 183
How Many You's? 184
Four Evermore 185
Quick Trick Game of 20 185
Increase Your Allowance 186
Great Memory 187
Birthday Math 188

14. KNICKKNACKS & ARTIFACTS 189

Silver Lantern 190

Quick Trick Penny Bookmark 191

Ice-Cube Candles...192

Mosaic Planters 193

Dip-Dyed Greeting Cards 194

Quick Trick This is a Stick-Up! 195

Your Own Portfolio 196

Colorful Clay Ornaments 198

Papier-Mâché Mask.......................................200

Marbleized Stationary....................................202

15. IT'S NOT ALL JUNK 203

Log Cabin 204

Découpage Tray 205

Streetscape 206

Quick Trick Unlost Glove Puppet 207

Stained-Glass Window 208

Recycled Crayons 209

Functional Artwork 210

Scavenger Mask 212

Junk Sculpture 213

RAINY DAY MENUS 214
INDEX 220

GETTING STARTED

IMAGINE it's a rainy day, a holiday, an at-home-with-a-cold day. There's no school, no piano lesson, no dance class, no team practice, and no family outing to shape the hours ahead. Great, you say, what are you going to do? Not to worry. This book is jam-packed with activities, so you'll always have plenty of creative ways to spend your time. There are games to be played and created, projects to do involving art and crafts, scientific experiments and magic tricks to be performed, and much more. Some of the projects will encourage the artist in you; others will teach you a skill. Some games use your energy; others stretch your mind. But they're all enjoyable, entertaining, and ready for you to explore.

Here are some suggestions to help you get the most out of this book:

MATERIALS TO COLLECT

- Paper towel and gift-wrap paper tubes
- Gift wrap scraps
- Fabric scraps
- Yarn
- Embroidery thread
- Buttons
- Craft sticks
- Wooden dowels
- Sequins
- Glitter
- Feathers
- Beads
- Odd game pieces
- Empty film cans
- Shoelaces
- Old greeting cards
- Broken costume jewelry
- Ribbons
- Small gift boxes
- Empty cardboard food boxes (from cereal or spaghetti)
- Plastic containers with tops (from margarine and yogurt)
- Disposable microwave dishes (from frozen foods)
- Egg cartons
- Dried beans and pasta
- Old magazines and catalogs
- Comics
- Coloring books
- Odd socks and mittens
- Empty plastic soda bottles
- Cardboard cartons
- Styrofoam blocks

■ The best way to prepare for rainy-day projects is to build up a supply of materials. Stockpile things like paper towel tubes, scraps of gift wrap, and buttons. Be on the lookout for castoff supplies—like large cardboard boxes and disposable microwave dishes—that you can recycle in projects. Take a look at the list in the box on previous page for ideas on what to collect. Make sure things are clean before you store them in a convenient place.

■ Almost all the supplies and tools you'll need for the projects are the kind that you are likely to have around the house. This list in the box at right let's you know what's nice to have on hand. Remember to replace supplies as you use them up. It's also smart to designate a convenient place to store your supplies so you can get them out and put them away easily.

■ Some of the activities in this book are short, others will keep you busy all afternoon. Some projects require supplies and equipment, others need only you and your imagination. Certain games need a little advance preparation, others can be played on the spur of the moment. A few of the activities—projects that require sharp knives, hammers,

SUPPLIES TO HAVE ON HAND

- Scissors
- Crayons
- Felt-tipped markers
- Poster paints and brushes
- Pens
- Colored pencils
- Erasers
- Rulers
- Tape measure
- Yard stick
- Glue
- Clear tape
- Masking tape
- Stapler
- Construction paper
- Typing or computer paper
- Old newspaper
- String

and stoves—require an adult assistant. But many are designed to carry out by yourself or with a friend. To make the activities the best they can be, all of them have been tested by kids.

■ For days when you have time for only a quick activity—one that needs no preparation and few materials and is easy to complete—there are Quick Tricks. These are sprinkled throughout the book. Look for them in the table of contents or find them as you browse through the book. And for days when you

have a lot of time on your hands, there are suggestions for groups of activities that you can work on together in the Rainy Day Menus (see page 214).

■ Before you begin an activity, read the directions from beginning to end so that you understand exactly what you're going to do. Some directions are open-ended; they give you suggestions but encourage you to come up with your own ideas. Other directions are like recipes and need to be followed closely.

Even though most of the activities use items you have around the house, make sure before you start that you have the materials you need for the project you want to do. A list of the items you need is printed with each activity. Be sure to check it when you read the directions.

■ This book contains a lot of games and activities for rainy days and Saturdays, but your imagination contains even more. These projects are meant to start you thinking up your own ideas for things to do on an idle afternoon. So use this book as your inspiration and get started!

—Linda Hetzer

BIG ADVENTURES

Adventures can be loud, zany escapades or calm, thoughtful retreats. They're a chance to create your own world and challenge yourself in the process. Sometimes you'll get so caught up in an adventure that you want the fun to go on forever. That's what's so great about a rainy day or a weekend: You can spend an hour on a favorite new activity . . . or pass the whole day in an entirely new world.

OPEN A
RESTAURANT

Have the fun of a night on the town without leaving your home! Transform your family's evening meal into a festive occasion by setting up a restaurant.

YOU ✂ NEED

Construction paper • Felt-tipped markers • Index cards • Pencil or pen • Glue • Scissors • Tape • Order pad or notepad

■ Pick a name for your restaurant. It can be silly or funny or tell your "guests" something about the style of the restaurant. Is your restaurant an elegant hideaway or a coffee shop? Is it in the city or the country? You can call it anything you like—Chez Taylor, Lee's Family-Style Restaurant, or Aunt Belinda's Down-Home Cooking.

Make a sign for the restaurant using construction paper and markers. Hang the sign near your front door or in the doorway to the dining room.

■ Design the menus. What are you going to have for supper? (See page 112 for a salad that's easy to prepare, if you're interested in helping cook the meal.) Give each dish a fancy title or name it after a friend or someone in your family. Meat loaf can be Terrine of Chopped Beefsteak or Josh's Meat Loaf Special. Macaroni and cheese can be Pasta e Formaggio or Tiny Pasta Tubes in a Creamy Sauce. To make a menu, fold a piece of construction paper in half.

On the front, write the name of your restaurant in marker and add any design you like. Write the evening's menu on a blank index card. Start with the appetizer, then list the salad, main course, and side dishes, and end with the dessert. Glue the index card to the inside of the folded construction paper, and you're set.

■ Prepare an order pad so you can take everyone's order at dinnertime. You can use a pad of paper or index cards or a folded sheet of paper.

Set the table to match your theme—if your restaurant is fancy, for example, you could use cloth napkins and put candles on the table. Whether your restaurant is fancy or casual, napkins folded into fan shapes make an impressive addition to the table (see Napkin Fan, at right).

■ Wear an apron while you take orders and serve dinner. (You can place a kitchen towel crosswise at your waist and tuck the top corners into your waistband.)

Offer the menus first. Then take the orders. Serve the food to your lucky patrons. You can join them to eat, then play waiter again to clear the table and clean up the kitchen.

NAPKIN FAN

A fan-folded napkin creates a festive mood for any meal.

1. If you're using a cloth napkin, fold it in half. If you're using a paper napkin—which comes already folded in quarters—open up one fold so that the napkin is folded in half.

2. Fold the napkin into 1-inch accordion pleats, leaving the last 4 inches unfolded.

3. Fold the napkin in half again, with the pleats on the outside.

4. Fold up the bottom left corner and tuck it into the pleats. Stand the napkin up and open the pleats to form a fan.

YOU NEED
• 1 napkin (cloth or paper) for each place setting

CAMP IN

How do you go camping without worrying about bears? Pitch a tent in your living room!

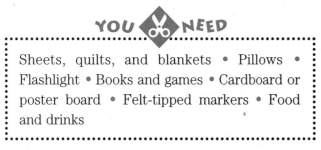

YOU NEED

Sheets, quilts, and blankets • Pillows • Flashlight • Books and games • Cardboard or poster board • Felt-tipped markers • Food and drinks

■ Drape old sheets or blankets over a card table, your dining room table, or three chairs placed in a triangle 4 or 5 feet apart, with their backs facing into the center. If you use chairs, make sure they are sturdy enough not to tip over when covered. Use an old quilt or blanket to make the floor of your tent, then add pillows, a flashlight, books, and games. You can even make trees for your campsite (see Trees, on the facing page).

■ Choose a name for your camp and make a sign. Fold a piece of cardboard or poster board in half (like a tent) and use markers

to write the name of your camp on the front. Set it up near your camp.

■ Since camping really builds up an appetite, you'll need a stash of tasty snacks to sustain you. Make Trail Mix by following the recipe on page 117. Put sandwiches, the trail mix, and a thermos of juice in your backpack and hike to your campsite for an afternoon of reading, games, and refreshments.

■ As the sun begins to set, hike to your campfire (the kitchen!). With some help from an adult "counselor," make some Banana S'mores (see page 124). Then enjoy the gooey treats as you reminisce about your day in the wilderness!

TREES
Make trees for your campsite.

1. Roll up several sheets of newspaper—wide sheets or tabloid size—and tape the roll closed.

2. From the top down, cut the tube into strips about 1 inch wide. Pull the strips down so that they resemble leaves.

3. Use poster paint to paint the leaves green and the trunks brown.

4. When the paint has dried, stand the trees up near your camp and use masking tape to anchor them to your "tent post" (a table or chair leg).

YOU NEED
- Newspaper
- Cellophane tape
- Scissors
- Green and brown poster paint
- Brushes
- Masking tape

HAVE AN
INDOOR PARADE

Get out your dress-up box and put together the most outlandish outfits you can create! The louder and more outrageous the colors and the bigger the clothing, the more fun you'll have creating the costumes. Use your own clothes, older brothers' and sisters' clothing, leftover Halloween costumes, and household items like doilies and bath towels. Try to include brightly patterned shorts, loud print shirts, brightly colored ties, out-of-style hats, colored knee socks, flowered dresses, plaid skirts, and striped blouses.

YOU NEED

Dress-up clothes • Cardboard cartons (optional) • Awards (see facing page)

■ Gather hats, wigs, scarves, and costume jewelry. For your feet, find sneakers, sandals, flip-flops, fuzzy bedroom slippers, and men's and women's dress shoes. If possible, divide what you've collected among four cardboard cartons,

two for clothes and one each for shoes and headgear.

■ Invite several friends to join you in creating outfits. (Ask them to bring over old clothes and accessories, too.) You can all parade around the room and then award prizes for the costumes: Most Colorful Costume, Silliest Costume, Cheeriest Costume, Costume That Used the Most Clothing.

Choose the categories for the awards ahead of time. Make sure you have enough categories so that everyone gets a prize. Make the awards before your friends arrive (see Awards, at right).

AWARDS

Reward your friends and have fun, too!

1. Draw 3-inch circles on construction paper by tracing around the bottom of a drinking glass. Cut the circles out.

2. For each circle, cut two 3-inch lengths of construction paper and notch one end of each strip. Glue the straight ends of the strips to the back of the circle.

3. Write the award categories on the circles with a marker.

4. To attach the awards, put a sticky-side-out loop of clear tape on the back of the circle.

YOU NEED

- Construction paper
- Pencils
- Drinking glass
- Scissors
- Ruler
- Glue
- Felt-tipped marker
- Clear tape

PLAN A
CARNIVAL

A sunny Saturday is the perfect time to put on a carnival to raise funds for a local day-care center or a community project. Why not spend a rainy afternoon planning the event?

YOU ❖ NEED

Paper • Pencils • Felt-tipped markers • Posterboard • Supplies for games and sales

■ Consult with parents—yours and your friends'—to decide where and when to hold the carnival, then make posters announcing it and hang them around your neighborhood. To make your posters enticing, feature the special attractions of the carnival, like games, a yard sale, a bake sale, and refreshments.

■ Fun is the first order of business. Decide on some games you can play on the sidewalk or driveway—like a beanbag toss (see Clown Face Beanbag Toss, on the facing page), horseshoes, ring toss, and bowling (see page 62). You may want to set aside a place for quiet pastimes, too, such as checkers or painting.

■ If you want to have a yard sale, ask friends and neighbors to donate outgrown toys, games, clothes, and other small items that are in good shape. Ask an adult assistant to help you figure out what to charge.

■ And finally, plan a menu for a bake sale. Choose foods that you and your friends can make easily and inexpensively with a little adult help, like cookies, brownies, Fruit Kebabs (recipe on page 114), bags of Trail Mix (recipe on page 117), popcorn, lemonade (during the carnival, keep the pitcher of lemonade in a bucket of ice).

■ Decide ahead of time what to do with the money you collect: Will any be used to reimburse the people who contributed food or will you donate it all to charity? To raise even more money, you could charge a small admission fee.

■ To make sure that all your friends participate—and no one's left out—divide the work so that everyone is in charge of one of the games or brings some food. Schedule half-hour shifts, with at least two people working each attraction at any given time. Ask a few adults to help out, too. Even though you and your friends will want to run some of the events, you should have lots of time to play the games and enjoy the carnival.

CLOWN FACE BEANBAG TOSS

Invite carnival goers to practice their pitch.

1. Turn a large carton upside down so the open end is on the bottom, then paint all four sides and the top in a bright color.

2. On one side of the carton, pencil in circles for eyes, nose, and mouth; they should be large enough for the beanbag to fit through easily when cut out.

3. Draw the rest of the clown face around the circles and paint it in. When the paint is dry, ask an adult to cut out the holes with a craft knife or box cutter.

4. On carnival day, each player gets three beanbags to toss through the openings. Hand out small prizes for each successful toss.

YOU NEED
• Large cardboard carton
• Poster paint
• Brush
• Pencil
• Craft knife or box cutter
• Beanbags
• Prizes

PRODUCE A TV SHOW

Do you have a favorite story that you think would make a good television show? Well, a rainy day is the perfect time to produce it. You can base your show on an original story—one that you or a friend wrote—or a novel, a short story, a poem, or even a popular song.

YOU NEED

Paper • Pencil • Costumes • Video camera (optional) • Paint, paper, sheets for making a set (optional)

■ First, adapt the story for television. Decide which part or parts would make a good episode and write up a brief summary, which would start something like this:

Two sisters, Emily and Elizabeth, live a pretty ordinary life until strange things begin to happen around their little town. They suspect the new boy at school of being behind the mysterious occurrences, since they started when he moved to town. What's more, Emily swears she's seen his golden retriever talking! But before pointing any fingers, the sisters decide to investigate. . . .

After you have the basics down, write a detailed outline of the action.

■ Make a list of the characters you'll need and who should play them. Does your story involve two young brothers who live alone, or is it about a large family: parents, children, a grandfather, an aunt, two cousins, and the next-door neighbors? Will you introduce other characters to keep the story moving, like a new baby brother or a long-lost uncle who suddenly shows up?

■ If you want to design sets and scenery, think about where your show takes place: Is it set in a tropical paradise like Hawaii or in a snowy New England town? In a palace or on a ship? Can you make a set for filming by painting a backdrop on an old sheet or a piece of butcher paper? Or are the kitchen table and a few chairs all you need?

■ What kinds of clothes do the characters need: bathing suits, pilots' uniforms, down parkas? If the story is set in the past, look at books that show the clothing of the time period for costume ideas. If the story takes place in the future, imagine what the characters would wear. Try to put some costumes together with things you and your friends have around the house.

■ Assign parts to your friends and family members and rehearse the show. Ask the actors to make up the dialogue according to the story line. The director—you or a friend—should guide the cast with constructive criticism.

■ Present the first episode in front of a live audience—other friends and family members—or tape it on a video camera and invite guests to a "screening" later.

This project could keep you happily busy for days or even weeks, if you decide to write a script and design elaborate sets and costumes. If the first episode goes well, you might even want to make a whole series.

TAKE A CRUISE...
OR RIDE THE RAILS

If your family has bought a large appliance or piece of electronic equipment that came in a large carton, or if you moved recently and have a large packing carton, don't let it go to waste. Use it to sail the high seas or go across the country by train.

YOU NEED

> Large cardboard carton • Craft knife •
> Masking tape • Felt-tipped markers • Old magazines • Construction paper • Glue • Snacks
> **FOR SHIP** • Long cardboard tube • Brown wrapping paper or butcher paper • Compass • Map • Paper-towel tube
> **FOR RAILROAD CAR** • Small cardboard box • Paper-towel tube • Paper plates • Bell (optional)

A Sailing Ship

■ To make a mast, use masking tape to tape one end of a long cardboard tube (the kind gift wrapping paper comes on) to the inside of the open side of the box, with most of the tube sticking up out of the box.

■ Cut a large triangular sail out of brown wrapping paper or butcher paper and decorate it with markers or stickers. Tape the sail to the mast.

■ To make your trip more exciting, make posters of foreign ports of call. Cut out pictures of exotic places—Tokyo, Singapore, Lisbon, Greenland—from old magazines and glue them to pieces of construction paper. Or draw your own posters. Write PARIS on your own drawing of the Eiffel Tower, THE NETHERLANDS on a photograph of tulips in bloom, IRELAND on a picture of sheep grazing on a hillside. Tape the posters around the room, and steer your ship toward them. (Check with your parents before you tape anything to the walls or furniture!)

■ Stock your ship with a compass, a map, a telescope (a paper-towel tube, decorated, if you like) and enough food to last until you see land. Then spend the afternoon sailing the high seas.

A Railroad Car

■ If you're a landlubber, turn the cardboard box into a railroad car. Tape a second, smaller box to the front of the big box for the engine. For the throttle, tape a paper towel tube to the inside front of the large carton. Next, decorate paper plates for the wheels and tape them along the sides of the boxes.

■ For travel posters for the train trip, cut out pictures of famous landmarks in the United States—the Golden Gate Bridge in San Francisco, the Statue of Liberty in New York, the Sears Tower in Chicago, the Alamo in San Antonio, the White House in Washington, D.C. Glue the pictures to construction paper.

■ If you have a bell, ring it along your route, as you call out the names of the towns and cities you are visiting. And don't forget the snacks to munch on until you reach your destination.

WAKE UP TO AN
OPPOSITE MORNING

On an opposite morning, everything's turned backward. It's best to prepare for the morning the night before by making sure everyone in your family knows it's happening. Opposite mornings are more fun when everyone agrees to go along. Here are some things you can do:

■ Start by getting ready for bed as soon as you get up. Get your next day's clothes out, brush your teeth, and read a bedtime story. When you walk, walk backward (carefully, of course, and not on staircases unless you hold on and go extra slowly).

■ When you get dressed, put your clothes on backward and inside out.

■ When you greet family members, say "good night" rather than "good morning."

■ When you set the table put the plate and glass face down with the fork on the right side and the knife and spoon on the left. If possible, turn the chairs backward.

■ Instead of breakfast, have dinner—how about spaghetti and meatballs?

■ When someone asks you a question, say "yes" when you mean no, and "no" when you mean yes. And every time you get angry at your younger brother and sister, give them a loving hug. How's that for opposite?!

Other opposite ideas:
- Read a short book from end to beginning.
- Sing a song backward.
- Play a game in reverse.

QUICK TRICK

HAVE A SING-ALONG

Music is a wonderful way to cheer up a dreary day and singing puts just about everybody into a good mood. Decide what kind of songs you would like to sing—current favorites, golden oldies, folk songs, show tunes, or maybe something silly, like Christmas carols on a warm spring day.

■ Arrange the seats in your living room, basement, or playroom in a circle so that everyone can sit together and see each other.

■ If someone in the family plays the piano or the guitar, ask them to accompany the singers. You can also write your own set of lyrics to a familiar song. This is called a parody and is lots of fun for birthdays and anniversaries.

■ For even more fun, try making up a song about your family vacation to the tune of "On Top of Old Smokey," or write lyrics about your Great-Aunt Sally's visit to a well-known tune like "She'll Be Coming 'Round the Mountain." Would you dare write a song about your *least* favorite person to the tune of "Ding, Dong, the Witch Is Dead" from *The Wizard of Oz?*

For refreshments after the sing-along, serve cookies (see page 120 for a recipe for Lemon Drop Cookies)—excellent with hot chocolate on a cold, wet day or with lemonade on a warm, rainy day.

PUT ON A
PUPPET SHOW

Stage a puppet show and invite your family, friends, and neighbors to watch. It's easy to set up the stage, make the puppets, and write a script.

■ For the simplest of stages, have the puppeteers kneel behind the living room or playroom sofa—move it out a few feet if it's against the wall—and raise the puppets over the top of the back cushions.

Or cover a large table—like your dining room table—with a sheet or blanket and kneel down behind it, raising the puppets over the edge of the table.

■ To make a tabletop puppet stage, you need a large cardboard carton. Ask an adult assistant to cut away the entire back and most of the front of the carton using a craft knife. Leave just enough front for a curtain area. Paint the curtain area, top, and sides of the carton with poster paint.

■ Now that the stage is set, write a script for the puppet show. It can be based on a book you have just read, an old fairy tale, a favorite mystery, or an original story.

■ There are many ways to make puppets. For realistic-looking puppets, you can draw the characters on paper or oak tag,

then cut them out and glue each one to a craft stick. For fantasy characters, use brown paper lunch bags. The bag slips easily over your hand and the bottom panel is a ready-made face. Draw on features with a marker, and add collage materials like feathers, sequins, buttons, bits of fabric, and paper scraps.

■ Now you're ready to make and send invitations to your friends. The invites can double as admission tickets (see Invitations, at right).

INVITATIONS

These invitations will serve as admission tickets, too.

1. Measure and mark 6- by-4½-inch rectangles on construction paper. (Or simply divide a standard piece of construction paper into quarters.) Cut them out.

2. Cut out half-moons from each of the short ends.

3. Starting from the middle of a half-moon, draw a dashed line across the center of the ticket. Above the lines write "Admit One."

4. In the middle of the ticket, write your invitation, including your name, the name of the show, and the date, time, and place of the performance.

YOU NEED

- Pencil
- Ruler
- Scissors
- Felt-tipped marker
- Construction paper

CREATE AN
ARTISTS' STUDIO

Invite your friends to join you in creating works of art in a studio that you set up in your basement, garage, or playroom. Later, you can exhibit your masterpieces in your own gallery.

YOU ✂ NEED

Newspaper • Art Supplies • Brown wrapping paper • Masking tape • Painting and drawing paper •Crayons •Colored pencils •Felt-tipped markers •Chalk •Oil pastels •Collage materials •Scissors •Glue •Index cards •Refreshments

■ Cover the floor of your "studio" with newspaper if you're working indoors, and divide the space into work areas.

■ First, set up one area for easels and poster paints. Make easels by taping plain brown wrapping paper to the walls, then taping paper to paint on in the center.

■ Arrange a drawing area, with paper, crayons, colored pencils, markers, chalk, and oil pastels.

■ Make a collage area. Provide all kinds of collage supplies: paper, fabric scraps, buttons, feathers, magazines to cut up, pipe cleaners, dried beans, pasta, glitter, sequins, and plenty of glue.

■ Let each artist choose the area they prefer and then create their work of art. If too many friends want to be in the same area at one time, set a half-hour time limit.

■ At the end of the time, have everyone change areas. After two rotations, everyone will have had a chance to work in each of the three art areas.

■ Later that day or the next day, after the room is cleaned up and the artworks are dry and hung on the wall, ask the artists to title their creations. Write each title and the artist's name and age on an index card and place it next to the artwork.

■ Once everything is ready, invite your friends and their friends and family to come to the opening of the art show. Serve juice and finger foods (cheese and crackers, pita bread and dip, or carrot and celery sticks are good choices) while people stroll around the room admiring the masterpieces.

BUILD A
HAUNTED HALLWAY

Whether it's close to Halloween or not, a gray, rainy day is the perfect time to set up a haunted hallway, a ghostly garage, or a panic-filled playroom for your friends to enjoy. After they walk through it, invite them to participate in a scary story, complete with gory details.

YOU NEED

Rubber gloves • Pantyhose • Spaghetti • Grapes • Licorice shoélaces • Potato chips • Dried apricots • Pudding • Plastic bag • Brown wrapping paper • Scissors • Black felt-tipped markers • Crepe paper • Dry leaves (optional) • Cassette recorder/player and audio tape of scary sounds (optional)

■ You can write your own scary story, tell one you remember from camp, or take out a book of scary stories from the library.

■ Gather the props you will need for the story, such as:

- a rubber glove filled with old panty-hose for a hand
- a paper bag filled with cold cooked spaghetti for intestines
- peeled grapes for eyeballs
- small pieces of licorice shoelace for toenail clippings
- potato chips for scabs
- dried apricots for ears
- for a heart, a sealed plastic bag filled with warm pudding (fill it just before you start)

If you'll be reading the story, put all the props, the book, and a flashlight in a box near where you will be sitting.

■ To decorate the walls of your haunted hallway, cut trees from brown wrapping paper. Make the branches spindly, and with a black marker, make the tree trunks gnarled and full of knots.

■ To attach the trees to the walls, fold pieces of masking tape, sticky side out, into loops. Place one side of the loop on the back of the tree and the other on the wall. Bend some of the branches so that they protrude from the wall.

■ Make ghosts that float from the ceiling (see Ghosts, on the next page).

■ Ask an adult assistant to tape crepe paper streamers to the ceiling, making them long enough so that the ends will brush against your friends' faces as they walk by.

■ If you're allowed, scatter dry leaves on the floor so that your friends will crunch on them as they walk around.

■ If you have a cassette recorder/player and an extra cassette, use it to make a tape of scary sounds. Fill it with weird laughs, creepy monster sounds, a witch's cackles, hooting owls, loud foot stomps, and any other scary noises you can think of. The tape should be at least 5 minutes long.

GHOSTS

**Make your haunted hallway *boo-*
tiful with these floating friends.**

1. Cover inflated balloons with white
plastic garbage bags. Gather the
garbage bag under each balloon to
form the head and tie it with a piece
of string.

2. Draw a ghostly face on the
garbage bag with black markers.

3. Use scissors to cut the bag
below the tie into shreds.

4. Tape another piece of string to the top of
the bag and have an adult assistant tape the
ghost to the ceiling.

  Make more ghosts and hang them with
different lengths of string so that the ghosts
hover at different levels.

YOU NEED
- Balloons
- White plastic garbage bags
- String
- Black felt-tipped marker
- Scissors
- Masking tape

■ Turn on the recorder right before your
friends arrive. Have them walk
through your haunted handiwork,
then seat them in a circle for the
frightening fun of your story.

■ Pass your props around as you tell
your tale to give everyone a real scare!

GAMES

We all know it doesn't matter who wins or loses . . . but a little friendly competition is a great way to liven up a humdrum afternoon. Some of these games can be played alone; others are best for a group. Some don't call for anything but brain work; others require you to build the playing board before you get started. But they're all fun. So round up some players and let the good times roll!

MAKE YOUR OWN BOARD GAME

If you love to play board games, why not create your own? This is a great way to research your favorite subject in school or your favorite hobby, since you have to make up all the questions.

YOU ✂ NEED

Oaktag or poster board • Pencils (black and colored) • Ruler • Felt-tipped markers • Index cards • Notebook or lined paper • Magazines • Glue • Scissors • Die

1. Choose a subject and make up a list of questions about it. For example, if you love dinosaurs, they could be the subject of a dinosaur game. Question categories might be different kinds of dinosaurs, their major characteristics, the foods they ate, and so on. If baseball is a favorite topic, questions could be about the players, the teams, the rules of the game, and famous plays. And if your passion is television, create a trivia game with questions about television shows, characters, theme songs, and the actors who played the roles. You'll need at least 40 questions.

2. To make question cards, cut index cards in half and write the questions on one side. Number the cards. Now, make an

answer book. In a small notebook or on several pieces of lined paper that you staple together, write the answers to the questions in the same numbered order as the questions.

If you know all the answers, the game won't be as much fun to play. So, to make the game more challenging, ask your parents or an older sibling or friend to write some of the questions with their answers.

3. For the game board, use a piece of oak tag or poster board about 11 inches by 17 inches. With a pencil, draw a wavy line—a series of curves and loops—from one end of the oak tag to the other. Draw another line parallel to and about 2 inches from the first. Divide this band into 30 or 40 boxes. If you are happy with the path of your game, make it permanent by going over the lines with a marker. Use colored pencils to lightly color the boxes in different colors.

4. Write START at one end of the playing path and FINISH at the other. Make several of the boxes "special instruction" squares. Leave enough empty squares between them so that the special instructions aren't all grouped together.

On two or three of the special instruction squares on the board write FREE TURN. ROLL AGAIN. On several other squares, write instructions that have to do with your particular game—HOME RUN! MOVE AHEAD 3 SPACES or STRIKE 3! MOVE BACK 2 SPACES, for a baseball game. For a dinosaur game, try T-REX ON THE PROWL! MOVE BACK 3 SPACES. Draw a place on the board for the pile of question cards.

5. For playing pieces, cut index cards in half, then fold them in half again to make "tents." Depending on the subject of your game, draw different dinosaurs, baseball players, or television characters on the cards, or cut out pictures from magazines and glue them to the cards.

6. To play the game, a player rolls a die, then picks up the top card. If the player answers the question correctly, he or she then moves the number of boxes indicated by the die. If the player answers incorrectly, the die is passed to the next player. When a player lands on a special instruction square, the player follows the special instruction without answering a question. The first player to reach FINISH wins.

CONNECT FOUR

This is a board game for two players. The object is to be the first to get your pieces in a row in any direction.

YOU NEED

Paper • Ruler • Pencil • Checkers or coins

1. To make the game board, draw a square divided into four identical boxes across and four boxes down on a piece of paper. Make each box large enough to hold a coin or checker. There should be a total of 16 boxes.

2. For game pieces use checkers or two different kinds of coins—pennies and nickels, for example. You need eight pieces in all, four of each color or kind.

3. Place four game pieces, arranged alternately, along the top row of boxes and four along the bottom row of boxes. (If you are using checkers, arrange them red, black, red, black. If you are using coins, alternate pennies and nickels.)

4. Sit opposite your opponent. One player moves only the red checkers and one moves just the black ones. (Or one moves the pennies and one the nickels.) Take turns moving one piece one box in any direction, even diagonally, without jumping over any pieces.

5. The winner is the first player to get his or her four pieces in a row in any direction—horizontally, vertically, or diagonally.

BOTTICELLI
JUNIOR

Botticelli is a guessing game for two or more in which the player who is It thinks of a person or character but reveals only the first letter of the character's name. (Decide in advance whether you'll use characters' first or last names.) The other players try to guess who the character is by describing him or her, and at the same time they try to stump the person who is It. Here's how the game works:

1. The player who is It thinks of a name, say Jo March, then gives the other players the first letter, in this case, J. The first guesser says, "Did you exchange your cow for magic beans and confront a giant?" The player answers, "No, I'm not Jack in 'Jack and the Beanstalk.'"

2. The second guesser says, "Did you defy your father and fly on a magic carpet?"

The player answers, "No, I'm not Jasmine in *Aladdin*."

3. The third guesser asks, "Did you jump over a candlestick in a Mother Goose rhyme?" The player says, "No, I'm not Jack in 'Jack Be Nimble.'"

4. The fourth guesser asks, "Are you one of the characters in a novel about four sisters who grow up during the Civil War in Concord, Massachusetts?" The player who is It says, "Yes, I am Jo March in *Little Women*," and the fourth guesser is now It.

5. If the player who is It stumps the guessers—if the guessers can't come up with any more guesses—then the player who is It reveals who the character is and wins the round. The next player then gets a turn at being It.

But, if during play, the player who is It is stumped by a decription given by a guesser, then that guesser becomes It. For instance, a guesser asks the player who is It, "Are you the little girl who tumbles down the hill with her brother?" If the player who is It cannot guess Jill (from the nursery rhyme), then the guesser becomes It (and the old It reveals who he or she was thinking of).

MOODY BLUE

This game can be played by two people or by a group.

■ Make a list of all the blue things you can think of in 2 minutes. Or if it's near Halloween, make a list of orange things. Or to make the game slightly more difficult, try thinking of gray things, or lavender things, or black-and-white things. See who can come up with the most items.

■ To score, cross off the items that everyone has listed, like the sky for a list of blue things, or a pumpkin for a list of orange things. You get a point for items you think of that other players (but not every other!) think of and two points if you're the only one who thought of an item. The person with the most points wins.

YOU DON'T KNOW
WHAT YOU'RE TALKING ABOUT

This game can be played by two or more people. The object is to stump your friends with convincing-sounding definitions for words they've probably never heard before.

YOU ❖ NEED

Dictionary • Paper • Pencils

■ If two people are playing, one player has a dictionary and chooses an unusual word, like *flotsam* or *plenipotentiary* or *contumelious*. The other player has 2 minutes to try to define or explain the word aloud.

The first player then reads the definition of the word from the dictionary. You can give points for defining words correctly, or you can just have fun learning some new words.

■ If more than two people are playing, tear a piece of paper into roughly even strips. Hand a strip of paper and a pencil to each player. Player One looks up a word that she thinks no one will know, reads it aloud, and writes the definition on a strip of paper.

■ The other players make up definitions, write them down, and pass them to Player One who reads each one aloud.

■ Each player then guesses at the right definition, scoring a point for a correct guess. Players also get a point if people guess that their made-up definition is the correct one.

■ Pass the dictionary around so that each player gets a turn to choose a word. After everyone has had a turn or two, the person with the most points wins.

I WAS AGHAST AT HIS THOROUGHLY CONTUMELIOUS BEHAVIOR

NAME THAT NUMBER

This guessing game is best for groups of three or more. To play, make up a list of word questions whose answers are numbers. Here are some ideas to get you started:

- Years in a decade
- Stripes in the U.S. flag
- Singers in a quartet
- Ounces in a pound
- Number that has 4 hundreds, 2 tens, and 13 ones
- Digits in a ZIP code
- Sides in an octagon
- Hours between 9:00 A.M. and 4:00 P.M.
- Toes on three feet (human feet, that is)
- Legs on a centipede
- Eggs in two dozen
- Players on a baseball team
- Pennies in a quarter, dime, and a nickel
- Inches in a yard
- First two-digit number

YOU NEED

Paper • Pencils

Have one person read the list, and let everyone else shout out the answers. Or make copies of the list, give one to each player, and have the players write down the answers.

You can play this game to see who finishes first, or you can just have fun finding the answers as a group. You can also keep score by giving out points for each correct answer; the player with the most points at game's end wins.

NIM SKILLS

Nim is an ancient math game for two players that looks easy but can be demanding. You have to think ahead and plan your strategy. Try a few games and see how challenging it is!

YOU ✂ NEED

20 small objects

■ Start with 20 objects—pennies, checker pieces, buttons, or small toys.

■ Each player takes a turn picking up at least one of the objects but no more than three of them.

■ The winner is the person who does *not* pick up the last object.

TWO-SIDED PUZZLE

A two-sided puzzle has a picture on both sides and is doubly challenging. To solve it, you first choose one picture to work on. Then you turn all the puzzle pieces so that that picture is facing up—or so you think! You may find as you fit the pieces together that you have to turn a few pieces over.

To make a two-sided puzzle, you will need two drawings of your own or pictures cut from a magazine or catalog and a piece of lightweight cardboard.

YOU NEED

Drawings or pictures • Cardboard • Scissors
• White glue • Pencils

1. Trim the pictures and the cardboard to the same size.

2. Glue one picture to the front of the cardboard and the other to the back. Let the glue dry.

3. With a pencil, lightly draw the shapes of puzzle pieces on your picture. To make the puzzle pieces, you may want to get ideas from the interlocking pieces of your favorite puzzle.

4. Cut the puzzle apart on the pencil lines. As you try to put the puzzle together, remember that each piece can be used on both sides. Part of the fun is deciding which side of each piece is supposed to be facing up.

MYSTERIOUS FUN

You don't have to be Sherlock Holmes to love a mystery. Whether it's in the pages of a book or on the silver screen, a mystery catches our attention and tantalizes us with a challenge. In this chapter, you'll discover what's cold and damp and hiding in a brown paper bag. You'll also see something that's hidden in plain sight. Hunt through old magazines for one game and comb the whole house for another. Write a message in code, then write one that disappears entirely. There's mystery in these games. See if they don't grab you!

INVISIBLE INK

When secrecy is all-important, write a note to a friend in disappearing ink. It will look like a blank piece of paper, but you both will know how to read it.

YOU NEED

Lemon wedge • Toothpicks • Plain white paper • Lamp with 100-watt bulb

■ To write the note, squeeze the juice from a lemon wedge into a small bowl. This will be the ink for your note, and a toothpick will be your pen. You'll have to dip the toothpick into the lemon juice quite often, probably before you write each letter, so start by writing a short message.

■ When you've written your note, set the paper aside for a few minutes to let it dry.

■ Give the note to your friend. To read it, she'll have to turn on a lamp with a 100-watt bulb and let the bulb get hot.

■ She should then hold the paper over the light without letting it touch the bulb. (Be careful—that bulb is hot!) Your secret message will appear in a just few seconds, as the heat of the bulb turns the lemon juice brown.

SECRET CODE

Communicate with your friends! Confound your enemies! Write in code! There are many kinds of codes, and it's fun to make one up.

YOU ✄ NEED

Lined paper • Pencil

■ One way to start is to substitute one letter in the alphabet for another. Fold a piece of lined paper in half the long way; in the left column, write the alphabet beginning with A.

Then choose a letter—say H—and write the alphabet in the right column as if H was the first letter—H, I, J, and so on. Write A after Z and end with G (the letter before H in the real alphabet). In this code, A=H, B=I, C=J, and so on. Using the code, you might write FVB HYL TF MYPLUK*.

If someone cracks your code, it's easy to make a new one. Change the letter that you start with, reverse the order of the "code" alphabet, or use random letters that don't have an obvious order.

■ You can also make a code by using a number for each letter, with A=1, B=2, and so on. In this code, you might write 12-5-20-19 7-5-20 20-15-7-5-20-8-5-18**.

*YOU ARE MY FRIEND. **LET'S GET TOGETHER

MYSTERY BAGS

Who knows what lurks inside that innocent-looking lunch bag? To play this game, you will need 10 paper lunch bags and 10 small, everyday household objects—a comb, a dry sponge, an old toothbrush, a small doll, a building block, an orange, a handful of fresh mushrooms, a marker, an audiocassette, a skein of yarn, a bicycle horn—anything that fits inside a lunch bag.

YOU ❖ NEED

Paper lunch bags • Household items • Felt-tipped marker • Twist ties or stapler • Paper • Pencils

■ Use a marker to number the bags from 1 to 10. Put one item in each bag and close the top, either with a twist tie or by folding it down and stapling it.

■ Pass out paper and pencils to all the players. Have each player gently feel the outside of each bag and then write down what he or she thinks is in it.

■ The object of the game is to guess the most items correctly.

HIDE IN PLAIN SIGHT

This game is a real-life version of "What's wrong with this picture?" Players try to spot common household items that are not in their usual places—like a toothbrush on a bookshelf.

YOU NEED

Household items • Paper • Pencils

■ Choose the hiding room. It should be one that's normally fairly neat so that out-of-place items can be spotted.

■ Choose 10 to 12 small objects that are unusual for the room—a baby photo, a coin, a hair bow, dishwashing liquid, and a greeting card, for example. Hide the objects in plain sight: For example, balance the coin against a vase of flowers, tuck the bow on a bookshelf, slip the greeting card partly under a sofa. No one should have to move anything to find the items.

■ Give the players paper and a pencil and have them list the items as they find them. Or give players a list of the items and have them check off each one as they discover it. The player who finds the largest number of objects in the least amount of time is the winner.

PASS IT ALONG

Like a game of charades, this game is played in teams. It is the most fun when at least six people play, with at least three players on each team.

■ Each team lines up, with players either sitting or standing.

■ The team that goes first decides what they will pass along. Will it be a piano? A feather? A crying baby? A hot slice of pizza? The funnier the made-up passed-along object, the more fun the game.

■ The first player on the team pretends to pick up the object using exaggerated motions, and passes it to the next player, who passes it to the next player.

■ The other team tries to guess what the object is. If the second team

QUICK ⏱ TRICK

FREAKY FOLDS

Take a piece of paper and try to fold it in half eight times. Challenge a friend to do the same.

Why can't it be done? Most people can fold it only six times because, after six folds, there are 64 layers of paper!

can't figure it out after three or four guesses, the first team reveals the object.

■ Then the second team thinks of an object and passes it along while the first team tries to guess what it is.

MAGAZINE
SCAVENGER HUNT

On a gloomy day, you'd have to go outside and risk getting wet if you were to do a real scavenger hunt. This one is best carried out on the sofa—with cookies to keep you going.

YOU ✂ NEED

Paper • Pencils • Old magazines or catalogs • Scissors • Construction paper and glue (optional)

■ To have a magazine scavenger hunt, first make a list of items you think you'll be able to find in pictures in the old magazines and catalogs you have on hand.

■ Depending on the type of magazines available, the list could include things like a new car, a movie star, a recipe, a smiling child, a map, a stereo speaker, work boots, a glass of milk, a fireplace, or a basketball player.

■ If you have friends over, divide into two or three groups and give each group a separate list. If you're playing with only one friend, each of you takes a copy of the list. The first group or person to cut out all the items on the list wins.

■ If you like, at the end of the game, you can give each player a piece of construction paper and some glue to create a collage using the cutouts.

BURIED TREASURE

Set up a treasure hunt with a real treasure at the end and clues that lead the players to it. If you want to participate in the hunt, ask an adult assistant to write out the clues and choose the hiding place.

YOU ✂ NEED

Gift-wrapping paper • Shoe box • Clear tape • Candy or small toys • Paper • Pencil

■ To make a treasure box, gift wrap the top and bottom of a shoe box separately, so that it's easy to open and close.

■ Put prizes (like candy or small toys) in the box and hide it somewhere in your house.

■ Plan a trail that will lead friends to the treasure—for instance, from the kitchen to the living room to the hall closet to the basement to the bathroom. Write clues that will guide the players in hunting.

■ You could write the clues in rhyme for added mystery. For example, for the first clue, you might write, "For a treasure box, look under the socks" and hide the second clue under the socks in the laundry room. For the second clue, you could write "If you want a hidden treasure, look near the screen of pleasure," and place the next clue near the television set.

■ You can make up as many clues as you want, but the seekers will probably be eager to find the box after six or seven. All who have searched for the treasure box get to share in the bounty.

STRING
FLING

Weave a belt or a friendship bracelet, make a giant spiderweb or a beautiful vase, create a basket or a piece of original art—all from ordinary household string or leftover yarn. Some of the projects in this chapter, like the yarn-covered vase, are quick to make, while others, like the woven belt and the twined basket, require more time. You can set up most of these projects and then work on them a little at a time until they are completed.

FRIENDSHIP BRACELET

A friendship bracelet is fun to make and give to your best friend. Bracelet making can sound confusing at first, but you'll learn all you need to know if you read through the directions carefully and refer to the illustrations before you begin. The bracelet takes only about 10 minutes to make. But first you have to set up the project and master the braiding technique. Plan to make it in one sitting, because if you take the loops of thread off your fingers, it is nearly impossible later to figure out which loop is which! And any change in loops will show in the pattern of the finished bracelet.

YOU ✂ NEED

Embroidery or cotton crochet thread • Measuring tape or ruler • Scissors • Tape

a

1. To make a bracelet, cut five 30-inch lengths of embroidery thread or crochet thread, three of one color and two of another.

2. Fold each of the five strings in half and tie them all together with an overhand knot (a) at least 2 inches from the cut ends. It's easiest to work on a flat surface, and the threads must be held tight, so tape the cut ends securely to a kitchen table or counter.

3. Separate the thread loops so that you have the three of one color on the left and the two of the second color on the right. With your palms face up, slip the loops onto your fingers—one on the pointer and middle finger of your right hand and one on the pointer, middle finger, and ring finger of your left hand (b).

LEFT **b** RIGHT

4. Slip the ring finger of your right hand through the first two loops on your left hand. With the right ring finger, hook the third loop (the one on your left pointer) by the outer strand (c)

RIGHT

c

LEFT

and pull it back through the first two loops (d). Now your right hand has three loops and your left hand has two. Pull your hands wide apart to tighten the braid (e).

5. Now move the two loops on the left hand over one position: The loop on the middle finger moves to the pointer and the loop on the ring finger moves to the middle finger, leaving the left ring finger free (f). Slip the left ring finger through the first two loops on your right hand.

6. Now hook the third loop by the outer strand and pull it back through the other loops on the right hand. Pull the loops taut.

7. The two loops on the right hand now move over one position: The loop on the middle finger moves to the pointer and the loop on the ring finger moves to the middle finger, leaving the ring finger free.

8. To braid, alternate these moves. Each time you complete a stitch, move both hands far apart to tighten it, then move the loops on the two-loop hand so that they're ready to make the next stitch.

Continue until the bracelet measures 6 inches. Tie an overhand knot in the loops at the end of the stitches and tighten it.

Like a friendship that's constant, a friendship bracelet is meant to be worn all the time, not taken off and put back on. When you put the bracelet on your friend's wrist, knot it so that the beginning and end knots lie next to each other. Make a double knot on top of this one and trim both the cut ends and the loops close to the knot.

STRING BALLOON

String balloons make wonderful decorations—they look like a cross between a spiderweb and a piece of modern art. You can make one using one kind of string or yarn or, for a different look, a mixture of all kinds: bakery string, kite string, household twine, crochet cotton, embroidery thread, and knitting yarn.

YOU  NEED

Balloons • Ruler • String • Scissors • Waxed paper • Masking tape • Petroleum jelly • White glue • Paper plate • Pencil • Safety pin • One or more kinds of string, yarn, or thread

1. Completely cover your table or work surface with waxed paper. Tape down the corners of the paper with masking tape.

2. Cut at least 30 pieces of string between 12 and 15 inches long.

3. Blow up a balloon and knot the end. Cover the balloon all over with a thin layer of petroleum jelly (like Vaseline).

4. Pour a small pool of white glue onto a paper plate. Dip a piece of string into the glue and place it on the greased balloon. Continue to dip pieces of string into the glue, and place them onto the balloon. Overlap and cross the strings until you can see as much string as balloon. Let the balloon dry all day (or overnight).

5. When the glue has dried, use your finger or the eraser end of a pencil to gently poke between the strings and push the balloon away from the strings. Break the balloon with a safety pin and pull it out through one of the larger spaces between the strings.

The hardened strings will hold the shape of the balloon. You can tie a long string to the string balloon and hang it from your ceiling.

MACRAMÉ
KEY CHAIN

A few half knots can make your average piece of string downright attractive. Use them to make a macramé key chain—for yourself or to give as a gift. The key chain has a loop that you can slip on your belt. The "chain" you make is long enough so that you can keep the keys tucked in your pocket.

YOU ✂ NEED

Twine or plastic lanyard • Measuring tape or ruler • Scissors • Round or clip-type key ring • Large-eyed plastic yarn needle • White glue

1. To make a 6-inch key chain, cut two pieces of twine or plastic lanyard: one 36-inch length for the inside cords and one 72-inch length for the outside cords. If you have never made half-knots before, you may want to make the inside and outside cords different colors to help you keep track of them.

2. Slip both pieces of string through the end of a key ring. Make sure the ends of each doubled string are even. Holding on to one long and one short cord in each hand, tie an overhand knot by putting the left cords over the right and putting the right cords through the loop, then pulling the knot tight. Arrange the cords so that the two long strands are on the outside and the short ones are on the inside.

3. With another piece of twine or lanyard, tie the key ring to the back of a chair or a doorknob so you can work with the cords held tight.

4. To start a half-knot, bring the left cord over the two center cords and under the far right cord (a). Then bring the right cord under the two center cords and up through the loop formed by the left cord (b). Tighten the knot by pulling on the left and right cords evenly (c).

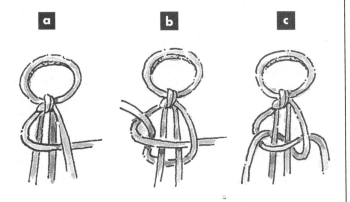

5. Continue to make half-knots until the length of knots measures about 6 inches. The knots will twist around the center cords. At the end, tie the inside cords together in a regular overhand knot just below the last half-knot (d).

6. To begin the loop, separate the cords into two pairs, made from an inside and an outside cord on the left and an inside and an outside cord on the right. Use each pair as if it were one cord. Make a 2-inch loop with the two pairs of cords and tie them together in a loose overhand knot (e).

7. Wrap the pair of cords on the left around the left half of the loop and wrap the right cords around the right side of the loop, wrapping the cords about three or four times (f).

8. Tie the pairs again in a loose overhand knot at the top of the loop (g). You now have a 2-inch loop of twisted cord.

9. Thread the cord ends—each one separately—into a large-eyed plastic yarn needle and tuck the ends under the twists of cord on the loop (h). Trim the ends close to the loop.

10. If you are using cord or twine, put a little white glue on each overhand knot at the top and bottom of the loop and on the cut ends to keep them secure. Be sure to let the glue dry before you use your key chain! If you are using lanyard, just tuck the ends into the loop and trim the excess.

QUICK TRICK

BRUSHLESS PAINTING

If the art bug bites you and you don't have a brush handy, grab a handful of string and paint a picture anyway! Here's how:

■ Put about 2 tablespoons each of different colors of poster paint into separate shallow dishes or paper plates and add 1 to 2 teaspoons of water to each dish.

■ Hold one end of a piece of string in each hand. Dip the center of the string into one color of paint. Holding the string taut, place it on a piece of paper, then lift it off.

■ Another way to paint with string is to hold only one end of a piece of string, dip it into the paint, drop it loosely onto the paper, and lift it off.

YOU NEED
• Poster paints
• Shallow dishes
• Water
• Paper
• String

■ In either technique, keep dipping and painting until you have a design you like. Use a fresh piece of string for each color. See how many different kinds of designs you can make using different string textures.

STRAIGHT CURVES

Would you believe that you can create graceful curves with straight lines? Here's how.

YOU ✂ NEED

Lightweight cardboard or paper plate • Ruler • Pencil • Hammer • Nail • Embroidery needle • Cotton embroidery thread or cotton crochet thread • Scissors • Construction paper or oak tag • Glue

1. On a piece of heavy paper or lightweight cardboard (a lightweight paper plate is a good size and weight), draw a 4-inch (or larger) square with a ruler and a pencil. Then mark off every ¼ inch along all four sides of the square.

2. To make holes large enough for a needle and thread, put the cardboard on a pile of newspapers and make a small hole at each mark by hammering a nail into the mark. Don't make holes in the corners of the square.

3. Thread a large-eyed embroidery needle with about 2 feet of cotton embroidery thread or crochet thread and make a knot at one end. (You will be working with a single thread.)

Working on the two adjacent sides of the square that form the lower left corner, bring the thread up from the back of the cardboard through the first mark on the far right in the bottom row.

4. Then, from the top, sew down into the bottom mark on the left row (a). Come up in the second mark on the left row and go down into the second mark on the bottom row (b).

Come up in the third mark on the bottom row and go down in the third mark on the left row (c).

5. Continue this way until you've used up all the marks in the two sides. Knot the thread on the back. Now, admire your handiwork. Every line you made with the thread is straight, but the result is a beautiful curve!

6. To continue, turn the square top to bottom so that the other two sides now form the lower left corner. Stitch it the same way you did the first.

7. If you would like to make a two-layer piece of string art, turn the square one quarter turn so that the two corners you have just finished become the upper left and lower right corners of the square. Stitch the new lower left corner the same way you did the first two. (You will be reusing holes that you used for the first two corners).

8. Turn the square from top to bottom and stitch the fourth corner the same way. You can use a contrasting color thread for the second two corners. Or try using a different color for each corner.

9. To display your string art, cut around it, leaving a ½-inch border. Glue the art to a piece of construction paper. Or, to make a sturdier frame, cut an 8- to 10-inch square of a coordinating color of oak tag and cut out a 4½-inch square from the center. Put glue around the border of your string art on the *front* and place the frame on top of it. You can decorate the oak tag frame or leave it plain to let the beauty of your string art shine through.

TWINED YARN
BASKET

Make a colorful basket for your desk to hold those loose things that always get lost: paper clips, rubber bands, and erasers.

1. First make the base. Cut a 1½- by 10-inch strip of corrugated cardboard (from a box or mailing carton). Fold the cardboard strip in half (so that the two shorter ends meet) and open it up. Now, fold each end into the center and open it up. You now have three folds making four equal sections.

2. With a ruler and a pencil, make a mark every ½ inch along each side. Since each side is 2½ inches long, marks will be at ½ inch, 1 inch, 1½ inches, and 2 inches. Each side will have four marks.

3. Form the folded cardboard into a square, with each fold a corner. Tape the open ends together with masking tape (making the fourth corner).

4. Now, bend eight 12-inch pipe cleaners in half, so that you know where the middle is, then open up the pipe cleaners. Push one end of a pipe cleaner through a hole in the top edge of the corrugated cardboard at the ½-inch mark and pull it through a little more than half way. Then push the end back up through a hole in the bottom edge at the 1-inch mark. Pull the pipe cleaner through so that the middle is against the bottom edge of the base and the ends, above the base, are even.

5. Take a second pipe cleaner and put one end in at the 1½-inch mark and the other end at the 2-inch mark. Repeat on each side of the base. You will have 16 spokes sticking up, four on each side of the base.

6. Now you're ready to start twining! You'll need 8 to 10 pieces of yarn, each 2 yards (6 feet) long. Take one piece, fold it in half, and slip the fold over any spoke.

7. Moving from left to right, twine around the spokes with the two strands of yarn, crossing the back yarn over the front yarn (a).

8. Continue twining this way, going over the corner spaces as well. When you come back to the spoke where you began twining, place the new row of yarn over the yarn in the previous row. As you go, push the woven rows down for a tighter weave. After a few rows, you'll see the basket getting rounder.

9. When you run out of yarn or want to change colors, fold another piece of yarn in half and slip the fold over the next spoke. Leave the ends of the old piece of yarn on the inside of the basket.

10. Continue weaving, changing colors as often as you like, until only 1 inch of each pipe cleaner is not covered. Tuck the ends of yarn into the weaving and trim off the excess.

11. To finish the top edge of the basket, fold each pipe cleaner into a loop. Tuck the end into the same space as the spoke (b).

12. To make the basket bottom, cut the cardboard at the corners (c). Be careful not to cut the yarn! Fold each piece of cardboard, with its loops of pipe cleaner, flat, in turn, tucking the end of the last flap under the first (d). You may want to ask an adult assistant to help you do this.

YARN-COVERED
VASE

Use up leftover yarn and recycle a plastic soda bottle to make a great-looking vase for paper roses.

YOU ✄ NEED

Plastic clean, empty 1- or 2-liter bottle (or other container) • Sandpaper • White glue • Yarn • Toothpick • Scissors

■ Cover a work space with newspaper. Roughen the outside of the bottle slightly with sandpaper. Put glue around the top of the bottle just below the neck. (By starting at the top of the bottle, any glue that runs down will not drip onto the yarn.)

■ Now, start wrapping yarn around the bottle. Use a toothpick to push each round of yarn close to the one above it. You want to cover the bottle completely with yarn.

■ To create a striped vase, change colors whenever you want. Simply cut off the yarn you are working with and glue the end to the bottle. Start the next color yarn right next to the cut end of the previous color.

■ To keep the "front" of the vase looking smooth, make all color changes on the same "side" of the bottle. Use that side as the back of the vase.

■ To make another design, use the glue to draw an outline on the bottle in the shape that you want. Then starting with the outside of the design, place yarn in the glue. Fill in the center of the shape with shorter pieces of yarn.

■ If your shape (or shapes!) is small, continue wrapping yarn around the bottle, going around the shape(s).

■ To wrap yarn around a large, central shape, cut the wrapping yarn so that the end lies right next to the shape and glue it down. Begin the wrapping yarn again on the other side of the shape. Bring it around the bottle and when you reach the shape, again cut the yarn and glue down the end.

■ Repeat wrapping and cutting the yarn until you reach the bottom of the shape. Then continue wrapping around the bottle until the bottle is completely covered with yarn. Let the glue dry.

■ For a variation, make a bud vase—a small vase meant to hold a single flower—by covering an 8-ounce plastic water bottle. Or cover an empty yogurt cup or other shorter, open container to use as a pencil holder.

PAPER ROSES

These roses will never wilt . . .

1. Cut tissue paper into 4- to 6-inch squares or rectangles. (The size and shape do not have to be exact.) You'll need four pieces for every rose you want to make.

2. Using all one color or two shades of one color or four different colors, stack four pieces of tissue paper one on top of the other, with the corners not matching.

3. Poke a hole in the center of the paper stack with the end of a pipe cleaner, and push the pipe cleaner through the hole.

To make a stamen in the center of the flower, make a 1-inch loop with the end of the pipe cleaner that's sticking up through the paper. Twist the end around itself.

4. Gather the tissue paper up and around the pipe cleaner to form petals. Wrap the pipe cleaner around the base of the petals to keep them in place. Arrange the petals until you like the way they look.

YOU NEED
- Scissors
- Colored tissue paper
- Pipe cleaners

YARN BELT

You can weave a good-looking cus-tomized belt using thick rug yarn or bulky knitting yarn. All you need is a sim-ple loom (of your own making) and a col-orful assortment of yarn scraps. (You'll need at least a couple of ounces.)

YOU ✄ NEED

Plastic straws • String • Measuring tape • Scissors • Bulky yarn • Clothespin

1. First, make a simple loom. Cut two plastic drinking straws in half.

2. Then cut four pieces of string, each piece twice your waist measurement plus 10 inches. (If your waist is 20 inches, your string pieces would be 50 inches long—20 + 20 + 10.) Fold each piece of string in half and push each folded end through a straw half so that a 2-inch-long loop sticks out.

3. Cut another long piece of string and slip it through the four loops. Knot it to make a ring large enough to slip over a doorknob (a). Attach this ring to a doorknob, a hook on the wall that's low enough for you to reach, or the back of a slat-back chair.

4. Tie the other ends of the strings to the back of a chair and move it far enough away from the hook or door (or other chair) so that the strings are straight and taut (b). Your loom is now ready!

5. To begin weaving, tie the end of the thick yarn to the pair of strings at the right. The tie should

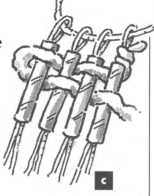

be up against the top edge of the straw (c). Now, bring the yarn under the first straw, over the second straw, under the third straw, and over the fourth straw.

6. For the next row, start from the left. Bring the yarn under the first straw, over the second, under the third, and over the fourth. Continue this way, always going *over* the straws you went *under* in the previous row and *under* the straws you went *over*. With your fingers, push each row firmly against the previous one.

7. When the weaving has almost covered the straws, gently pull them down on the string below the section you've woven and continue weaving over the straws (d).

8. When you run out of yarn or want to change color, do it in the middle of a row. Leave the end of the first color under a straw and bring the second color up over the next straw. You can tuck the stray ends into the woven belt when you have finished, using a knitting needle or chopstick. (If you want to leave the weaving and come back to it later, use a clip-type clothespin to attach the yarn to the string. This will keep the weaving in place until you return to it.)

9. When the belt is long enough to tie around your waist, tie the yarn to the far right or far left pair of strings. Untie the strings from the chair and remove the straws.

10. To keep the belt from unraveling, tie each set of strings in a knot right against the end of the weaving. Then knot one string from the first set of strings to one string from the second set, knot the second string from the second set to one string from the third set, and knot the second string from the third set to one string from the fourth set. You can leave the strings as fringe or trim them and tuck them into the weaving.

11. At the beginning end, cut the large loop and slip it out. Then cut each of the four 2-inch loops and knot the strings the same way you did on the other end. The belt is now ready to tie around your waist.

MINIATURE GOD'S-EYE

Originally created by the Huichol (pronounced WEE-chohl) Indians of northwestern Mexico as symbols of the power of the unknown, god's-eyes are popular decorations, and today they are considered good luck symbols. The Huichol Indians are pantheists—they believe god is everywhere in nature. The four points of the cross that forms the frame of a god's-eye represent earth, fire, air, and water. In making a god's-eye, the Huichol Indians offer a prayer that a particular spirit might watch over them.

YOU  NEED

Craft sticks • White glue • Ruler • Yarn • Scissors • Toothpick

1. To make a miniature god's-eye, center one craft stick on top of another at right angles to it. Put a dab of white glue where they meet. Let the glue dry.

2. Cut several 18-inch lengths of yarn in one or more colors. Holding an end in place where the two sticks meet, wrap one of the lengths around the center of the sticks and back across the opposite way, forming an X (this holds the yarn end in place).

3. Then wind the yarn over, under, and around each craft stick in turn (a). You can work clockwise or counterclockwise, whatever's most comfortable. Make sure each wind is pushed tightly against the one before it.

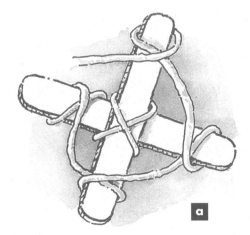

a

4. When you want to change colors, knot the first color at the back of one craft stick. Start the next color on the next craft stick, knotting the yarn at the back of the stick (b).

b

5. When you finish wrapping your god's-eye, knot the end of the yarn. On the back, use a toothpick to put a dab of glue on each yarn end and press

the ends flat to keep them secure. To hang the god's-eye in your room, tie the two ends of a piece of yarn to one of the wraps of yarn on the back of one craft stick (c). Secure it with some glue and let the glue dry. Hang the loop on a nail or hook in your room.

c

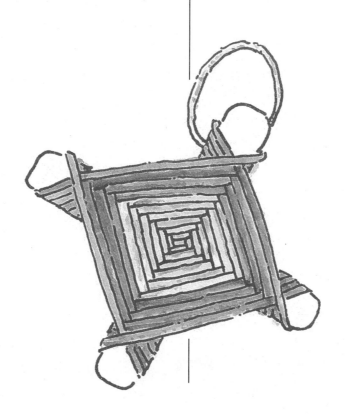

YARN SPIDERWEB

Spin a spiderweb in your playroom or basement with a leftover skein of yarn. But warn people before they come in the room—or they may get an unwelcome lesson in how spiders catch their prey!

YOU NEED

Yarn

■ Start by tying the end of the yarn to a chair or door handle, then wind the yarn around and over everything in the room until you have used it up.

■ If you have a friend visiting you, use two skeins of yarn in different colors and, working together, wind them both around the room. You can crawl in, around, and under the spiderwebs.

■ When it is time to take the spiderweb down, untie your finishing end and begin to wind the yarn into a ball. (Be sure to remember where the end is!)

■ If you and a friend made webs, switch colors, so you undo his web and he undoes yours. Work carefully so that the two colors of yarn don't get tangled. Find your way back to the starting point, winding as you go. And save the yarn for another rainy Saturday!

INDOOR
SPORTS

If rain puts a damper on sports and games, why not bring them inside? But before you mark out an end zone with Mom's matching Ming vases, remember that you'll have to change your games slightly to suit your surroundings. Make indoor play a little less rowdy, and use softer equipment so that friends aren't hurt and furniture isn't damaged. Since your basement or playroom is much smaller than the playground, you'll want to play games that call on your skills more than your muscles. Save football for a sunny day.

MINIATURE GOLF

If miniature golf is a favorite Saturday afternoon activity, don't wait for a sunny day to play. You can make your basement or playroom into a miniature golf course.

YOU NEED

Kids' golf clubs or a new sponge and a yard-stick • Masking tape • Felt-tipped marker • Ball • Oatmeal container • Shoe box • Cardboard • Coffee can

■ If you have a set of kids' golf clubs, use them. If you don't, you can make your own by attaching a stiff new sponge to the end of a yardstick with masking tape. Use a regular golf ball or a small rubber ball and a doormat for the tee.

■ Make eight or ten obstacles for the course. Here are some ideas to help you get going.

- For a tunnel, cut out the bottom of an empty oatmeal box and place the box on its side.
- For a house, turn a shoe box upside down and cut out an entrance from one end of the box and an exit from the other end.
- Fold a piece of cardboard in half and set it up like a tent for the ball to go through.
- For a ramp, take a large piece of cardboard and score it in two places to divide it into thirds. To score, run one point of a pair of scissors along the cardboard. Ask an adult assistant to help you. Bend the cardboard slightly at the score marks and place the center portion on a book. Angle the two ends to form sloping ramps.
- Place two or three Frisbees on the floor to form a curved fairway for the ball to go through.
- For a straight fairway, make two parallel rows of building blocks.
- Use a hula hoop to make a sand trap that you want to avoid.
- Put a chair or stool in the center of the room for the ball to go under.
- Use an empty, clean coffee can placed on its side as the end cup.

■ Set up your obstacles around the room and use masking tape to secure them to the floor. Write numbers on the masking tape to indicate hole numbers for the course.

■ Start at the beginning and see how many strokes it takes to get your ball through the course and into the coffee can at the end. Don't forget you're indoors, so use more finesse than force when you tee up.

BOWLING

Bowling is a sport you can play with any size group in any large, clear space—the playroom, the basement, your bedroom, even the hallway—if you use lightweight game pieces.

10 empty plastic 2-liter soda bottles • Ball • Pencil • Paper

■ For the pins, use 10 clean empty plastic soda bottles set up in a triangle: four in the back row, three in the next row, two in front of them, and one in the first row.

■ For the bowling ball, use a toddler's large rubber ball, a foam ball, or a beach ball.

■ Put a piece of masking tape on the floor at least 10 feet away from the pins. Players get two rolls on

each turn to knock down all the pins. The pins must be set up again after each turn.

■ Everyone gets 10 turns. Score a point for each pin you knock over.

■ If you roll a strike (knocking down all the pins with the first ball in a turn), you score 10 points plus a 15-point bonus. Then it's the next player's turn.

■ You score a spare when you knock down all 10 pins in two rolls (one turn). The score for a spare is 10 points plus a 10-point bonus.

■ The winner is the player who has the highest number of points after all the players have completed 10 turns.

BALLOON VOLLEYBALL

Spike! Play a version of volleyball that doesn't require an actual net.

YOU NEED

Rope or clothesline • Balloons

■ Clear a playing court, and the area around it, by moving any breakable items, such as lamps and knick-knacks, out of the room.

■ Place a length of rope or clothesline across the floor in the middle of the room to indicate sides.

■ Blow up a balloon to use as a volleyball. Then you and your friend (or friends) divide up and swat the balloon back and forth across the line.

■ A team gets a point if the balloon hits the floor on the opponent's side or if an opponent fails to hit it back over the string to the opposite side in three tries.

■ For a really lively game, inflate balloons in two different colors— say red and blue—and play with both at once. One team gets a point each time the red balloon hits the floor on the opponent's side; the other team scores with the blue balloon.

WASTEBASKET BALL

If shooting hoops is your passion, here's a way to set up a game in the house so that you can practice your jump shots.

YOU NEED

Paper grocery bag • Newspaper • Masking tape • Laundry basket, wastebasket, or cardboard carton

■ Make a basketball by stuffing a large brown paper grocery bag half full with crumpled sheets of newspaper. Fold over the top of the bag and seal it with masking tape. Mold the bag with your hands until it is rounded, then put additional masking tape all around it to help keep its shape. You've made your basketball.

■ For the basket, put a plastic laundry basket, wastebasket, or empty cardboard carton on a chair at one end of the room. Stand 6 feet from the chair and see how many baskets you can make.

■ If you have friends over, take turns shooting baskets from a range of distances—6 feet, 8 feet, 10 feet—if there's enough room.

■ If you want to keep score, give two points for baskets made from up to 8 feet away and three points for baskets made from farther away.

QUICK TRICK

CUP CATCH

Cup catch is quick to set up and easy to play!

■ Give each player a large paper or plastic cup to use as a mitt.

YOU NEED
• Paper or plastic cups
• Aluminum foil

■ Make a small ball out of crushed aluminum foil.

■ Toss the ball back and forth, using the cups to both toss and catch the ball. No hands allowed!

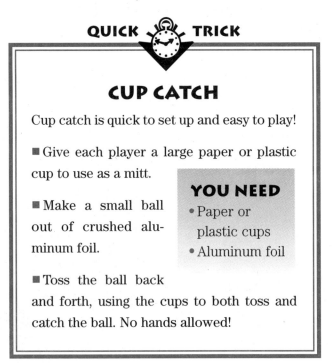

OBSTACLE COURSE

You never know when you'll find yourself in some far-flung jungle or desert faced with a breathtakingly deep gorge or high mountain. How will you get around it? Best to start training for future adventures now, with an obstacle course. Set one up in your basement or playroom.

YOU ✂ NEED

Stool • Hula hoop • Shoe boxes • Cardboard carton • Building blocks • Jump rope

■ Think of things that will challenge you—make you stretch that arm, extend that leg, and pull up those knees! Here are a few suggestions:

- climb up on a small stool
- jump into a hula hoop balanced on two shoe boxes
- crawl through a large cardboard carton with the bottom cut out
- walk on a building-block balance beam
- jump with a jump rope
- climb over a dining room chair that's lying on its side

■ If friends are over, choose one as the leader and let everyone else follow. Then let each person take a turn leading the group through the obstacles in a different order.

SKEE BALL

The game of skee ball, a cross between bowling and tossing a ball at a target, is often played at arcades and county fairs.

YOU  NEED

Yogurt containers, large plastic cups, or empty shoe boxes • Masking tape • Old ball

■ To make a skee ball field of your own, tape together six containers of the same size in three rows—three in the first row, two in the second row, and one in the third. You can use empty yogurt containers or large plastic drinking cups with a small ball or empty shoe boxes with a larger ball. Use an old small rubber ball or tennis ball—one that doesn't have much bounce left in it.

■ Put the taped-together containers flat on the floor and stand several feet away.

■ Score 10 points for getting the ball in one of the containers in the bottom row, 20 points for one in the middle row, and 30 points for the top container. The person with the highest score after 10 throws is the winner.

QUICK TRICK

SARDINES

Sardines is a twist on the game of hide-and-seek. All the players close their eyes, but only one person hides. On the count of 10, everyone starts to search.

■ When you find the person who is hiding, you join her in the same place. More and more players squeeze in as fewer players are left searching. The last person to find the hiding place is the hider in the next game.

■ Choose safe places to hide; no locking closet, cabinet, trunk, or wardrobe; no place near breakable items or chemicals, like cleansers or solvents. If you choose a closet, leave the door slightly ajar to be on the safe side.

A DAY AT THE RACES

Sometimes, you can race against just one other person, but it's much more fun to divide a group of friends into two teams and run relay races. Here are 10 different races—for two people or for teams.

YOU ✂ NEED

TISSUE PAPER RACE: Straws, tissue paper.
PAPER PATH RACE: Construction paper, tape.
DRESS-UP RACE: Oversize T-shirts, boxer shorts, rubber gloves.
BALANCING BALLS: Big spoons, tennis balls.
CHEERIOS CHALLENGE: Uncooked spaghetti, Cheerios.
PASS THE ORANGE: Oranges.
POSTURE WALK: Books.
BALLOON RACE: Balloons.
SHOE BOX SHUFFLE: Shoe boxes.

■ **Tissue paper race.** Blow through a drinking straw to keep a small square of tissue paper aloft as you walk from the start to the finish line.

■ **Paper path race.** Tape pieces of construction paper (masking tape works best) to the floor to make two paths. The paths should be far enough apart to keep racers from colliding, and the sheets of paper only a step apart—a *big* step won't hurt. Race by stepping from one piece of paper to the next. Your feet cannot touch the floor—they must always land on a piece of paper. You can set up the pieces in a straight line or, for more fun (and silliness), arrange the pieces in curving paths. Just be sure to use the same number of pieces in each path, to keep the race evenly matched.

■ **Dress-up race.** Place an oversize T-shirt, a pair of boxer shorts, and a pair of rubber gloves on each of two chairs at one end of the room. Players run to the chairs and put the gloves on first, followed by the T-shirt and shorts. Then they quickly take off all the clothes and run back to the starting line.

■ **Balancing balls.** Hold a tennis ball on a large soup spoon as you run to the finish line and back. Hand the spoon to the next player on your team without dropping the ball. If you drop the ball, start your turn again. See which team finishes first.

■ **Cheerios challenge.** Hold an un-cooked strand of spaghetti between your teeth. Slip a Cheerio onto the spaghetti and keep it there as you race-walk to the finish line.

■ **Pass the orange.** Tuck an orange under your chin and pass it along to the next person on your team (who must take it with his chin) without using your hands.

If you drop the orange, start your turn again. See which team finishes first.

■ **Posture walk.** Race-walk to the finish line balancing a book on your head.

■ **Balloon race.** Race to the finish line holding an inflated balloon between your knees.

■ **Shoe box shuffle.** Put a shoe box on each foot and see who can shuffle across the room the fastest.

■ **Frog race.** Squat down and jump like a frog from the start to the finish line.

SCIENTIFIC
STUFF

Can you cause a volcanic eruption? Capture your shadow? Hear sound waves traveling through wood? See around corners? Yes. All you need are some materials you probably already have around the house—and a little bit of curiosity. Just remember to follow some basic rules: Read the experiment directions carefully before you begin so you understand exactly what to do, line up an adult assistant for the experiments that require one, and clean up your work area when you're finished. And most important, have fun experimenting!

BLOW YOUR STACK

So it's not exactly Mount St. Helens! You can still watch a volcano erupt in your kitchen. Make the volcano in a 12-ounce plastic soda or water bottle. (Liter bottles don't work nearly as well—the smaller bottle, the better the eruption.)

YOU ✂ NEED

Measuring spoons • Baking soda • Measuring cup • Water • Dishwashing liquid • Plastic bottle • Newspapers • Distilled vinegar • Food coloring (optional)

1. Stir 1 tablespoon of baking soda into ¼ cup of water and pour the mixture into a plastic soda bottle. Add a couple drops of dishwashing liquid.

2. Put the bottle on the floor on top of a pile of newspapers (or in your kitchen sink) and carefully add ¼ cup distilled vinegar, keeping your face away from the top of the bottle as you pour. Watch the eruption.

3. For more drama, add a couple drops

of blue or red food coloring to the water. But be careful with this exotic eruption—food coloring can stain kitchen surfaces and your clothes.

HAIRY HARRY

Watching seeds sprout is always thrilling, but when the sprouts are green hair, it's even more fun.

YOU ✄ NEED

Milk or juice carton • Sharp knife • Ruler • Pencil • Construction paper • Clear tape • Felt-tipped markers or crayons • Potting soil • Radish seeds

1. To make Harry, wash out a 1-quart milk or juice carton. With a sharp knife, cut it in half so that the bottom piece is about 4 inches high. (Ask an adult assistant to help cut the carton.)

2. Draw a 4- by 12-inch rectangle on a piece of construction paper and cut it out. Wrap the paper around the carton, and secure it with tape. Use markers or crayons to draw a face for Harry on the paper, making sure that the top of the carton is at his hairline.

3. Put potting soil in the carton to a height of about 3 inches. Then sprinkle radish seeds over the soil. (Radish seeds are available at gardening stores and five-and-tens.) Push the seeds into the soil about ½ inch deep and water them lightly.

4. Place Harry on a windowsill and check him every day, watering him if he gets dry. Radish seeds sprout quickly. In 3 or 4 days, Harry will be hairy.

PERISCOPE UP

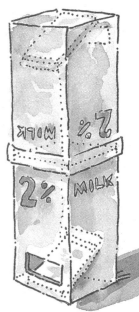

Do you want to see around corners? Don't let anatomy stop you! Build a periscope—an instrument that allows you to see things that are not in your direct line of sight. You're probably familiar with the periscope on a submarine that lets the sailors see what is on top of the water when the submarine is under the surface. Here's how to make one for dry land.

YOU NEED

Two half-gallon size milk or juice cartons • Scissors or craft knife • Two small mirrors • Masking tape

1. To make your own periscope, cut off the tops of two clean half-gallon milk or juice cartons with scissors or a craft knife. Ask an adult assistant to help you with this.

2. Ask an adult assistant to help you cut a viewing hole about 2 inches wide

by 1 inch high in one side of each carton 1 inch from the bottom edge.

3. Tape a small mirror (about 1½ by 2½ inches) reflective side up, at a 45-degree angle in the bottom of each carton opposite the viewing hole.

4. Tape together the open ends of the cartons so that the viewing holes are on opposite ends and opposite sides of your periscope.

5. To use your periscope, stand near a fence, bookcase, or any object that is taller than you but low enough so that the top of the periscope sticks up above it.

Or, stand near a door, holding the periscope horizontally, and look through the opening.

ELECTROMAGNET

You know that magnets can pick up metal objects. Do you know that you can create a magnet by having electricity move through a simple nail? This is called an electromagnet.

YOU ✂ NEED

> Bell wire • Scissors • D-cell battery • 3-inch nail • Tape • Small metal objects

1. To make an electromagnet, remove about 1 inch of the covering from each end of 2 feet of bell wire by gently cutting the covering with scissors—you don't want to cut into the wire—and peeling it off. Ask an adult assistant to help you. (You can buy bell wire at either a hardware or a variety store.)

2. Stand up a D-cell battery so that the positive end (marked +) is the top and the negative end (marked –) is the bottom.

3. Tape one end of the wire to the side of the battery, leaving enough exposed wire free to reach the positive end at the top.

4. Wrap the wire tightly around the length of a 3-inch nail, leaving 1 inch of the nail exposed at the tip. Bring the other end of the wire to the bottom of the battery. Tape the bare wire at this end to the negative charge at the bottom.

5. Holding onto the covered part, touch the bare end of the wire to the top (positive) end of the battery. This allows electricity stored in the battery to flow through the nail, "turning on" the magnet. (The bare end of the wire will get hot, so be careful.)

Try to pick up paper clips, safety pins, straight pins, nails, and screws with the exposed tip of the nail. See how many you can pick up—and watch them tumble when you break the connection!

KITCHEN GARDEN

Start a conservatory on your windowsill. Use a rainy morning to plant dried lima beans, fresh carrots, parsnips, or potatoes, and fruit. All these will grow into beautiful plants with leaves and stems, but they will not produce more vegetables or fruits.

YOU NEED

Vegetables and fruit seeds • Drinking glasses or glass jars • Paper towels • Toothpicks • Flowerpots • Vermiculite (available in garden and variety stores) • Potting soil

Lima Beans

Line a clear glass tumbler with a damp paper towel. Put dried lima beans between the glass and the paper towel. Check the towel each day, adding water to keep it moist; in about a week you will see sprouts.

A Carrot or Parsnip

Cut off about ½ inch of the top of the vegetable and place this piece flat side down in a shallow dish. Pour in enough water to almost cover the vegetable top.

Alternatively, you can place the vegetable top in a flowerpot filled with vermiculite, a growing material for plants.

Place the flowerpot on a plate. Pour on just enough water to  moisten the vermiculite. Keep the dish or flowerpot in a dark place—a cupboard or a closet. Add more water each day. Within a couple days, you'll see sprouts. Move the pot into the light. When the plants grow larger, replant them in larger pots with potting soil.

A White or Sweet Potato

Put three toothpicks into the center of a medium-size potato and place the potato in the opening of large drinking glass or jar so that the toothpicks rest on the top edge.

Put enough water into the glass or jar to cover the bottom of the potato. Place the glass or jar in a sunny window. Add water each day to keep the bottom of the potato in water. You should see sprouts and roots in about a week. If you like, you can then plant the potato in a flowerpot with potting soil.

Orange or Apple Seeds Peach Pits

Rinse the seeds or a pit in warm water to remove any remaining pulp. Pat dry with a paper towel. Fill a small flowerpot to within ½ inch of the top with potting soil. Push one peach pit or about six seeds ½ inch into the soil. Pour in enough water to dampen—not soak— the soil.

Put the pot in a plastic bag. Keep the bag loose and secure the open end with a twist tie. Put the pot in a dark place—a cupboard or a closet—until you see sprouts, usually a couple of weeks.

Take off the plastic bag, water the plant, and put the pot in a sunny place. Check the soil every few days and add water when the soil is dry.

EDIBLE SPROUTS

Grow sprouts you can eat in a salad or sandwich!

1. Put a clean, wet kitchen sponge in a glass bowl, and sprinkle the sponge with seeds like alfalfa, soybean, wheat, barley, sesame, or mung beans.

2. Cover the bowl tightly with clear plastic wrap. Depending on the type of seeds you used you'll see sprouts in 2 to 5 days.

3. When the sprouts appear, remove the plastic wrap, put the bowl in a sunny place, and spray the sprouts with water every day. They'll be ready to eat in 5 to 7 days.

YOU NEED
- Kitchen sponge
- Glass bowl
- Assorted seeds
- Plastic wrap

CAPTURE
YOUR SHADOW

When you're outside in the sunshine, you often see your shadow. Sometimes, usually around the middle of the day when the sun is high in the sky, your shadow is short and close to your body. Other times, usually late in the afternoon when the sun is low, your shadow is long and thin. It's hard to play with your shadow on a rainy day, so here's how to create one indoors.

YOU NEED

Lamp • Masking tape • Paper • Pencil • Black construction paper • White glue • Butcher paper or brown wrapping paper • Black paint • Brush

■ Move a lamp away from the wall—to the center of the room, if possible—and remove the shade so that the bulb is bare. Place yourself between the lamp and the wall. Do you see your shadow on the wall? Can you make it change shapes or sharpness by moving back and forth?

■ To make a silhouette—an outline of the side view of your face—tape a large piece of paper to the wall (get an adult's permission before you do this). Stand in front of it sideways so that the shadow of your profile fills the paper. Have a friend trace the outline of the shadow.

■ Take the paper off the wall and cut around the outline. Trace it onto black

construction paper, cut it out, and glue the black silhouette onto a piece of white paper. You've captured your shadow!

■ To make a life-size body tracing, tape a very large piece of butcher paper or brown wrapping paper to the wall and stand farther away from the light source so that your entire shadow, from head to foot, is on the paper. Have a friend trace around your body. Fill in the body tracing with black paint and let it dry.

QUICK TRICK

DOLLAR BRIDGE

Rest a crisp, new $1 bill on two upside-down paper cups or small glasses so that only about 1 inch of each end rests on the glasses or cups. Have a quarter in your hand. Ask a friend if he can balance the quarter on the dollar. He may try different ways, but it won't work! The dollar is not strong enough to support the quarter. Now, tell your friend that you can balance not only one quarter but four quarters on the dollar bill. Here's how.

YOU NEED
- $1 bill
- Two paper cups or small glasses
- Four quarters

■ Fold the dollar in half lengthwise, then fold each long edge to the center fold. Place the folded bill on the two glasses with the center fold facing down. The groove made by the center fold faces up.

■ Slowly and dramatically, place in the groove first one quarter, then the next and the next, until you have balanced all four quarters in the groove.

■ Why does it work? By folding the dollar bill to form grooves you have created a strengthened dollar "bridge" that can support greater weight. The folded dollar bill is like corrugated cardboard used for shipping cartons that is stronger than a flat sheet of cardboard.

FEED THE BIRDS

Putting food in your backyard for birds is a kind gesture, and it attracts birds for you to watch from your windows. Making a bird feeder on a rainy afternoon will bring you and your family hours of pleasure once the sunshine returns.

YOU NEED

Sharp knife • Orange or grapefruit • Spoon • String • Skewer • Bird food

1. To make the holder, cut a large orange or a small grapefruit in half. Scoop out the fruit from one half and save the other piece for a snack. Then use a skewer to punch three evenly spaced holes in the skin, around the circumference of the hollowed-out half, about ½ inch from the cut edge. (Ask an adult assistant to help you cut the fruit and skewer the holes.)

2. Cut three 18-inch lengths of string and tie them all together at one end in a knot. Center the bottom of the fruit on the knot. Bring one string through each hole in the fruit (from outside to inside), and then knot the ends together at the top.

3. Make the bird food (see the box on the next page) and pack it in the center of the holder. When the rain stops, hang the bird feeder from a tree branch that is strong enough to hold it and that is not too close to your house. (You don't want the birds flying into your windows.)

The birds will come to depend on the food that you are providing, so be sure to check the feeder from time to time and add more food as needed.

BIRD FOOD

Whip up a tasty feast for your feathered friends.

½ cup creamy peanut butter
1 cup cornmeal
¼ cup sunflower seeds or birdseed
⅛ cup raisins (optional)

Mix all the ingredients together in a small bowl, then serve to your backyard birds.

QUICK TRICK

BATH CENTS

Would you like all your pennies to look shiny and new? You can make them that way by giving them an overnight bath.

■ Put ⅓ cup distilled vinegar and 1 teaspoon salt in the bottom of a drinking glass and stir to combine. Add eight or ten tarnished pennies. Leave the glass on the kitchen counter overnight.

YOU NEED
- Drinking glass
- Measuring cup
- Measuring spoon
- Distilled vinegar
- Salt
- Spoon
- Pennies

■ The next morning the pennies will shine. Do you know why? The vinegar and salt chemically combine to become a cleaning solution for copper pennies.

TABLETOP
TERRARIUM

A terrarium is like a tiny greenhouse. You can create one in a large glass bowl using small plants that you buy, harvest from your backyard, or have grown from vegetables (see page 74). A tabletop terrarium requires supplies that you probably don't have around the house. So if the weather report calls for rain this weekend, visit a garden shop, variety store, or pet store during the week to get what you need.

YOU ✂ NEED

Glass bowl • Gravel or pebbles • Charcoal •
Potting soil • Plants • Stone, shell, or figurine
(optional) • Plastic wrap

1. To make the terrarium, put some small pebbles or fish tank gravel in the bottom of a large glass bowl, and then add a sprinkling of charcoal, which is also called activated carbon and is available in pet stores.

2. Put a 2-inch layer of potting soil on top of the gravel and charcoal. Make holes in the soil with your fingers and put in the plants, making sure the roots are covered with soil. Water the soil until it is damp but not wet. Add an unusual stone, a pretty shell, or a figurine to the bowl, if you wish.

3. Cover the bowl with clear plastic wrap, sealing it tightly. Put the terrarium where it will get daylight but not direct sunlight.

How does your garden work without regular watering? Because the top of the terrarium is sealed, water doesn't evaporate. It cycles—it goes from the soil to the air and back again to the soil.

RAINWATER
WATCHING

What could be more appropriate for a rainy day than having a close look at rainwater? To perform the experiments shown here, put a bucket outside to catch some rainwater—or just use tap water from the kitchen sink.

Breaking the Tension

Water tension is like an invisible film or skin that covers the top of water. It is formed because the water molecules on the surface of water are more attracted to the other water molecules below them than to the air above them.

YOU NEED

Water • Glass or small bucket • Small floating items • Dishwashing liquid

■ To see water tension at work, put some water in a glass or small bucket. Gently place small, lightweight items that float—like a leaf, a piece of paper, or a small safety pin—on top of the water. Keep adding items until the weight becomes so great that the water tension breaks and the items drop into the water.

■ Now, add a couple of drops of dishwashing liquid to the water and try the same experiment. What happens? Why do you think the items drop into the soapy water sooner? The dishwashing liquid has already broken the water tension before any objects are placed on the water.

The Unbroken Circle

YOU NEED

Soup bowl • Water • Thread • Bar of soap

■ For another experiment with water tension, fill a soup bowl with water. With a 6-inch length of thread, make a long, thin loop, overlapping the ends of thread. (See the illustration on the next page.) Do not knot the thread ends. Place the loop gently on top of the water in the bowl.

■ Now, touch the end of a bar of soap to the water in the middle of the loop. What happens? The loop widens to a circle around the soap. Why? The soap has broken the water tension inside the loop. (The thread keeps the soap from going beyond the loop.) The water outside the loop still has tension, so it pulls away, drawing the thread with it to form a circle.

Hot and Cold

Which faucet leaks more, the one for the hot or the one for the cold?

YOU ★ NEED

Two paper cups • Straight pin • Two clear juice glasses • Cold water • Ice cubes • Hot water

■ To find out, make a tiny pin hole in the center bottom of each of two paper cups and place the cups on top of two clear juice glasses. Fill one cup with cold water and ice cubes. Fill the other cup with hot tap water.

■ Now watch the juice glasses. What happens? Water drips quickly from the hot water cup but slowly or not at all from the cup of cold water. Why? The molecules in the hot water move faster than those in the cold water, fast enough to slip through the hole in the bottom of the cup.

QUICK ⏱ TRICK

LASSO AN ICE CUBE

Float an ice cube in a glass of water and put a piece of string next to the glass. Ask a friend if he thinks he can pick up the ice cube with the string. What do you think he will do? He'll probably try to tie the string around the ice cube, which is just about impossible. You can show him an easy way to do it.

■ Place the string on top of the ice cube and sprinkle salt lightly over it. Then wait a few minutes.

YOU NEED
• Ice cube
• Glass of water
• String
• Salt

■ The salt will make the string stick to the ice, and you'll be able to lift the ice cube right out of the glass.

High and Low

Want to see water move from one glass to another all by itself?

YOU NEED

Two drinking glasses • Box • Water • Handkerchief or two paper towels

■ Put a drinking glass on the table and another glass on a box next to the first glass. Fill the glass with water. Can you get the water to go from the glass on the box into the glass on the table without pouring it in? Of course you can!

■ Twist a handkerchief (or two paper towels together) into a long, tight roll. Put one end of the twist into the water in the glass on the box and put the other end into the glass on the table. What happens? In a minute or so, the water soaks into the handkerchief and begins to drip into the bottom glass.

If you wait long enough—go away and come back after you've played a game or had lunch—you will see that almost all of the water from the high glass has flowed into the low glass.

83

GOOD VIBES

Turn one of your friends into a "psychic"—someone who can mysteriously read your mind.

■ You need a table made of wood. Sit at one end of the table and have your "psychic" friend sit at the other. Have a second friend stand behind the "psychic."

■ Tell the standing friend that the seated one can tell him how many fingers he holds up, even though she can't see him.

■ Here's how it works: The seated player puts her head down so that her ear is against the table. When the standing player holds up, say, three fingers, you scratch the underside of the table (gently—be sure not to tap) three times.

■ The scratching sound travels through the wood to the ear of the "psychic." Sound waves actually travel better through wood than through air! The seated player counts the number of scratches she hears and then calls out the correct number of fingers.

THE FAMILY HISTORIAN

Every family is unique. Learning about your own can be fun and surprising—it may even teach you something about yourself. So don't hesitate to ask: *What was it like for Grandpa Dave to be a soldier? What does Great Grandma Anna mean by the "old country"? How did your parents meet? And exactly why is Aunt Norma's nickname Cookie?* When you discover the answers to these kinds of questions (and others of your own), you may find your own family even more interesting than the one in your favorite sitcom!

READ ALL ABOUT IT!

Extra! Extra! Baby Andrew Takes First Step! Grandma Ruth Celebrates 60th! A newspaper filled with hot-off-the-press family news and neighborhood events is fun to create, and a rainy day is perfect for putting one together.

YOU  NEED

Blank paper or newsprint • Pencil • Ruler • Typewriter or computer paper • White glue or rubber cement • Photographs or other illustrations

■ First jot down ideas. What is some current family news? Did your dog have puppies? Did your class take a trip? Was your brother's school report on dinosaurs a success? Did your sister's soccer team win the tournament? Did your family have a picnic supper at a local park? You can write all the articles yourself, or you can assign some to family members.

■ Each story has to have a title, called a headline. If different people write the stories, make sure the writer's name appears under the headline—this is called a byline.

■ The easiest way to write a newspaper story is to answer the 5 W's—the *who*, *what*, *when*, *where*, and *why*—of an event. For example, for a story about your sister's soccer tournament, *who* is your sister, *what* was the soccer tournament, *when* was it, *where* was it held, and *why* was it held?

■ You can use photographs of family members to illustrate some of the stories, or you can draw your own cartoons and pictures.

■ Some newspapers also have special features, like a crossword puzzle, jokes or funny stories, movie reviews, recipes, and horoscope predictions. Special features can be a lot of fun to write!

■ To make your newspaper, you use a large piece of blank paper or newsprint. Work with the paper lengthwise for a full-size newspaper. To make a tabloid, fold the paper in half with the fold on the left side.

■ At the top center of the first page, write the newspaper's title. You can use your family's name in the title—the TOSHIRO TIMES or the GATEHILL GAZETTE—or create another name that would have meaning to your family. Put the date and the day's weather at the top of the first page, too.

■ Most newspapers divide their pages into columns. You can divide yours into two or three equal columns by drawing a light pencil guideline.

■ On typewriter or computer paper, either type or print out your stories to a width that's slightly narrower than your columns, then cut them out. Some stories are short and will fit in less than a column. Longer stories may take up more than one column.

■ Before you paste down your columns of type, decide where you want to place the photographs or drawings. Don't forget to put a caption under each one! Then add your cartoons and other special features.

■ When you have arranged all the items, paste them onto the newspaper with white glue or rubber cement. If some of your columns are not full, you can add a joke, riddle, or funny family anecdote to fill the space.

■ You can make photocopies of your newspaper at your local copy shop. Or if you have a computer and printer at home, you can create your newspaper on screen and print it out. Send copies to faraway grandparents, cousins, aunts and uncles, and friends. They'll be glad that you took the time and effort to create a newspaper about your family.

A DAY IN THE LIFE
OF YOUR FAMILY

Forget the Brady Bunch. Watching your own family on TV is much more fun. Make a video of a typical Saturday around your house to send to friends or relatives who live far away—or just to watch at home with friends.

Before you begin, ask each family member to think of things to say and do that show off their personalities. For example, one person may eat oatmeal every day for breakfast; someone else can never find her shoes; another person collects baseball cards. Urge family members to be themselves and you will produce a realistic as well as entertaining video.

YOU NEED

Videocamera • Videotape

■ Start with waking up. Who's up first (after you, that is)? Who's groggy and who's cheerful? Then, move on to breakfast. Who makes the meal? Who leaves the messiest place mat? Did anyone wind up with a milk mustache? What happens next? Does anyone have to do yard work? Walk the dog? Wash the car? Show your favorite activities—playing ball, jumping rope, playing board games. Who helps make dinner? What are your family's favorite foods? What's bedtime like?

■ If you don't want to make this just a typical Saturday tape, record different parts of the day on different days instead. That way others can see how you get ready for school, how the adults prepare for the work day, and what goes on in your family on a typical weekday.

RELATIVELY TRIVIAL

Here's a great way to get to know your family better—or just embarrass everyone! Create a trivia game with questions about your family members and special family events.

YOU ✄ NEED

Index cards • Pencil • Prizes (optional)

■ Write the questions on one side of index cards and the answers, upside down, on the other. One person can create the game, serving as sort of a family historian by coming up with all the questions and asking other family members for the answers.

Or you can give each family member—including your grandparents, aunts, uncles, and cousins—a few index cards and ask them to come up with five or six questions and to write the answers on a separate sheet of paper.

Here are some sample questions to get you started.

- Who tells the best jokes at family gatherings?
- Where was Mom born?
- What is Grandpa's nickname?
- Whose favorite dessert is lemon pie?
- Where did Aunt Judy go to college?
- What happened at the annual picnic at Lake George?
- For what did Uncle Greg win a national prize?
- Who is the dog named after?

■ To play the game, shuffle the cards and place them, question side up, on a table. Each player, starting with the youngest, takes a card and tries to answer it. Keep playing until all the cards have been used.

■ To keep the playing lively, award a token prize—a small candy, a box of raisins, or a small toy—for each correct answer. Or keep score on paper and award a grand prize—a day when the winner's chores are done by the other family members—to the high scorer.

INTERVIEW
YOUR GRANDPARENTS

Chances are, your grandparents have had fascinating lives—after all, the world has changed a lot since they were born. What were their lives like long ago? The next time they come for a visit, ask if you can interview them. If they live far away, maybe you can conduct the interview over the phone or by mail. (Ask your parents before phoning, because a long conversation can be pretty expensive.)

YOU NEED

Pencil • Paper • Cassette recorder and tape (optional)

■ Use a tape recorder, if possible, to record the conversation. Or write down questions on a piece of paper beforehand and then fill in the answers as you talk. Here are some questions to get you started.

- Where were you born?
- Did you live in a house or an apartment?
- What's your earliest memory?
- Where did you go to school?
- What were your favorite games and sports when you were young?
- Did you ever get into trouble?
- What were your chores around the house?
- What did you do in your free time?
- Do you still have friends from your childhood?
- Who was the funniest person in your family?
- What was your favorite place in your neighborhood?
- What was your favorite food? Your least favorite?
- What was your favorite holiday and how did you celebrate it?
- What kind of work did your parents do?
- How did you meet Grandpa (or Grandma)?
- What was your wedding like?
- If your grandparents were born in another country, be sure to ask about the food, customs, and clothing of that

country, and when and why your grand-parents emigrated.

■ Later, you can write stories from your tape or notes of your grandparents' memories. Then ask your grandparents to double-check them to make sure they're accurate. Put a cover on the pages and give the booklet a title—for example, *Grandma's Book of Memories*. Then, make copies and give one to each grandchild, as well as to your grandmother.

SPECIAL EVENT
ALBUM

You can make a special event in your life, or your family's, even more special by commemorating it in an album. The event can be anything—the school play in which you had a part, your sister's graduation from high school, your grandmother's 75th birthday—as long as it's meaningful to you or the person you're giving it to.

YOU  NEED

Package of self-adhesive pages for a photograph album • Construction paper • Plain white paper • Felt-tipped markers • Pen • Scissors • Yarn or ribbon

■ Collect photos and other mountable memories from the event. Depending on the event, these mementos can be ticket stubs, restaurant napkins, hotel stationery, postcards, or theater programs.

■ Ask family members to write down their feelings about the event—your grandfather's love for his "birthday girl," the feeling your sister had when she was handed her diploma, your thrill at being on stage for the first time—to include in your album.

■ You can make an album many different ways. A simple way is to use a package of self-adhesive photo album pages. This will protect the photos and other mementos under plastic. Make a construction paper cover page that includes the title and date of the event and a design, if you like. Put the cover page under the plastic on the first page.

■ Make a sample layout: arrange the photographs and other elements in order. Write a caption on plain white paper for each one, telling who is in the photograph and what they are doing. Include your thoughts, too. Use the captions to explain what the ticket got you in to see or what the food was like in the restaurant whose napkin you saved. Cut out the captions and put them below each photograph. Remember to include the written memories as well.

■ When you're pleased with the arrangement, lift the plastic sheets and put the items in place on the pages. To bind the book, thread yarn or narrow ribbon through the holes on the left side of the pages and tie it in a bow.

A BOW TIE
WALL HANGING

This unusual way of displaying small photographs of you and your brothers and sisters makes a great gift for your parents or grandparents. It's a ribbon wall hanging with framed photos attached.

YOU ✂ NEED

Wide ribbon • Scissors • Twist tie • White glue • Soda can ring tab • Needle • Thread • Photographs • Oak tag • Pencil • Ruler • Decorative trimmings

■ To make the bow, you will need about 1½ yards (54 inches) of 2½-inch-wide ribbon. Cut the ribbon into one 21-inch length (for the bow loops), one 10-inch length (for the center wrap), and one 18-inch length (for the section that hangs down from the bow).

■ To make the bow, first make a loop by overlapping the ends of the 21-inch length of ribbon about 2 inches. Cinch the center of the loop with a twist tie, securing the overlapped ends (a). Wrap the 10-inch piece of ribbon around the twist tie at least twice (b), glue it at the back, and trim the excess ribbon. Glue one end of the remaining ribbon to the back of the bow. Cut a V-shaped notch out of the bottom end to make the ribbon look fancy (c).

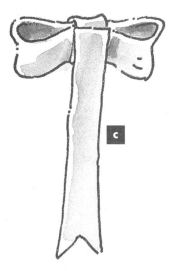

■ To make a hanging loop, sew on a ring tab from a soda can at the top back of the bow: Thread a needle with a sewing thread, double it, and knot the ends. Make small overhand stitches along the bottom of the ring (d).

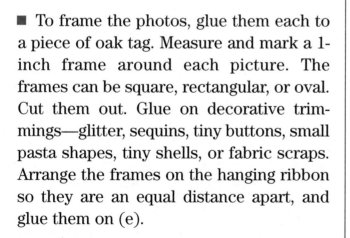

d

e

■ To frame the photos, glue them each to a piece of oak tag. Measure and mark a 1-inch frame around each picture. The frames can be square, rectangular, or oval. Cut them out. Glue on decorative trimmings—glitter, sequins, tiny buttons, small pasta shapes, tiny shells, or fabric scraps. Arrange the frames on the hanging ribbon so they are an equal distance apart, and glue them on (e).

FRAME YOUR FAMILY!

Put your favorite family photograph in a frame covered with fabric that matches your bedroom or living room. Here's how to make one for a 5- by 7-inch picture.

1. Start with a piece of medium-weight or corrugated cardboard at least 9 inches long by 11 inches wide. Draw a 5- by 7-inch rectangle in the center. Draw another rectangle that's 2 inches longer at both top and bottom and 2 inches wider on each side, than the first one around its border.

2. Ask an adult assistant to help you and cut around the outer rectangle with a craft knife. Then cut out the center rectangle. You should now have a 2-inch-wide frame.

3. Use cotton balls or quilt batting to make a cushioned frame. If you are using cotton balls, glue them all around one surface of the cardboard. If you are using quilt batting, ask an adult assistant to help you cut it to fit the cardboard, then glue it down (a).

4. Trim ½ yard of printed fabric to 13 by 15 inches. On the back (unprinted side) of the fabric, use a ruler and pencil to measure and lightly mark out a 5- by 7-inch rectangle in the center. Then draw diagonal lines from corner to corner of the small rectangle, to form an X. Cut along these lines to create four triangular flaps.

5. Place the fabric printed side down on your table and position the cardboard in the center of the fabric with the cushioned side facing down. Make diagonal cuts at the corners to eliminate the excess fabric.

Trim the triangular flaps of fabric in the center of the frame to 2 inches (b).

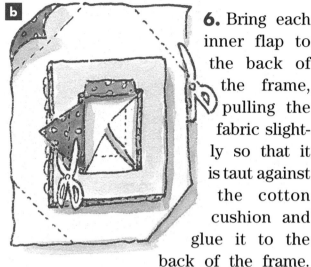

6. Bring each inner flap to the back of the frame, pulling the fabric slightly so that it is taut against the cotton cushion and glue it to the back of the frame. Do the same with the outer flaps. Gather the excess fabric at the corners and secure it with lots of glue. Let the glue dry.

7. Place your photograph in the frame, facing out through the opening, and tape it in place at the back.

8. To make a stand, measure and cut out a 3- by 13-inch strip of cardboard. Score the strip by holding a ruler 2 inches from the end and running one point of the scissors along the ruler. (Ask an adult assistant for help with the scoring.)

Glue the outside of the scored end of the stand to the back of the frame at the center of the top border (c). Let the glue dry before standing the frame on this strip.

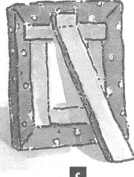

GROW A FAMILY TREE

What kind of tree can grow for hundreds of years without any water? A family tree, which records a family's members over many generations. It is usually presented as a chart, sometimes one that actually looks like a tree!

YOU NEED

Index cards • Heavy paper • Felt-tipped markers • Watercolors (optional) • Brushes (optional)

■ To make your family tree, gather information about your family. Begin with yourself (and your siblings and first cousins) and work backward to your parents, aunts and uncles, grandparents, great-aunts and great-uncles, and finally, great-grandparents. Go back further, if you can.

Find out each person's name (first, middle, and last, if possible); the date and place of his or her birth and death (if applicable); the name of the spouse, if any, and the date of the marriage; and the names and birth (and death) dates of any children.

■ Then, list the information for each person on a separate index card like this:
Name:
Date born:
Birthplace:
Married:
Date died:
Place of death:
Children's names:

■ On a table or the floor, put the cards in order, with you and your sisters and brothers at the top, your parents underneath you, and their parents underneath them. If you have information about your great-grandparents, put that on the very bottom. Make room for your aunts and uncles and their spouses, and include their children, too—they're your cousins!

■ Now that you have the information in order, you can draw your family tree. Your eight great-grandparents are the tree's roots, your four grandparents, the trunk, and your parents and any aunts and uncles, the branches. You and your siblings and your cousins "grow" from these branches—you can put each of these names on a separate leaf. If you have a lot of names, you might want to sketch out your tree first, then draw it on heavy paper. Once you've got all your family information on it, decorate the tree with felt-tipped markers or watercolors.

■ If this sounds too complicated, try working with just your immediate family: Start with yourself and record information about your parents, grandparents, and great grandparents. But skip your aunts, uncles, and cousins.

Put a title on your drawing—THE JOHNSON FAMILY TREE or MY FAMILY—and display it in your bedroom or den.

A FAMILY PHOTO ALBUM

You can keep family photographs in an album with plastic sleeves or self-adhesive pages that you buy at a variety or department store, but a photo album that you make yourself makes a truly unique gift for your family. A handmade album will keep your family's photographs neat and easy to look at.

YOU  NEED

Oak tag • Ruler • Pencil • Scissors • Fabric • Hole punch • White glue • Colored and black construction paper • Felt-tipped markers • Yarn or ribbon • Adhesive photograph corners • Self-stick labels (optional) • Large-eyed plastic yarn needle (optional)

1. Measure and mark two 9- by 12-inch pieces of oak tag to make the album covers. Cut them out.

2. On each sheet, measure 1 inch in from one short side and draw a vertical line with a pencil. Ask an adult assistant to help you score each line: Hold a ruler firmly against the line while you carefully run one point of a pair of scissors along the ruler's edge. The side with the score will be the inside of each cover.

3. In the center of the 1-inch area between the score and the edge of the oak tag, make a mark 1¼ inches from the top of the oak tag. Then make three more marks, each 2¼ inches below the previous one.

With a hole punch, make a hole at each mark. Ask an adult assistant to help. Do this for both pieces of oak tag.

4. Now cover the oak tag with fabric. To make the front cover, place a 13- by 16-inch piece of fabric printed side down on the table. Spread glue evenly on the front of one piece of the oak tag (the side without the score), then center it, glue side down, on top of the fabric. Turn the oak tag over and smooth out the fabric so there are no bubbles or wrinkles.

5. Turn the oak tag over again and trim the excess fabric at each corner, cutting it at an angle (a).

6. Put glue along the edges of the back of the oak tag. Fold over the excess fabric first at the top and bottom edges, then along the side edges. Put plenty of glue at each corner and gather in the fabric.

7. Trim a piece of colored construction paper to 8 by 11 inches. For the inside of the front cover, center and glue this paper to the back of the oak tag. Let the glue dry.

8. Feel for the holes you punched in the oak tag and mark the fabric over each one. Use the point of the scissors to carefully poke through the holes. Repeat steps 4 through 7 with the second piece of oak tag to make the back cover, making sure that the holes on each side align.

9. You can decorate the front cover any way you like. To make a nameplate, measure and mark a 2- by 5-inch rectangle on construction paper. Cut it out and round off the corners. Write the name of your album on it and glue it to the cover.

10. For the album pages, use 20 to 30 sheets of heavy black 9- by 12-inch construction paper. Make a mark 1¼ inches from the top left corner of the short edge. Then make three more marks, each 2¼ inches below the previous one on each sheet of paper, to match the holes in the cover. Punch holes where marked.

11. To assemble the album, make a neat pile of the construction paper pages. Place the pages on top of the inside back cover, then place the front cover on top of the pile. All the holes should line up.

12. Use 1 yard of yarn or ribbon to bind the album together. It may help to use a large-eyed plastic yarn needle. Starting from the back, bring the ends of the yarn or ribbon through the center holes, then go down into the end holes. Thread the yarn or ribbon up through the center holes again and tie the ends in a bow at the front. Trim off any excess (b).

Use adhesive photograph corners to secure the photographs to the black paper pages. (You can buy them at a camera sup-

ply store or a variety store.) *Never* use glue or rubber cement to hold photographs, since they cause deterioration. If you want to make identifying captions, write them on small white self-stick labels and place them below the photographs.

NEAT
TREATS

On a rainy day, the best treats are quick to prepare, fun to make, and great to eat. Here are several recipes that are just that! You'll find that making them is easy when you follow step-by-step directions. You can make a sweet treat like Chocolate Crunch Bars for an after school snack, prepare a healthy Mixed Green Salad with Vinaigrette Dressing to add to your family's dinner, or surprise everyone with fluffy Popovers for Saturday morning breakfast.

KITCHEN BASICS

- Before you begin, prepare by reading through the entire recipe so that you know what you'll be doing. Then get out all the ingredients and utensils you will need.

- Make sure an adult is available to help you with knives, electrical appliances such as blenders and electric mixers, and the stove burners and oven.

- Wash your hands and wear an apron or smock when preparing food.

- After you've finished cooking, be sure to clean up and put everything away.

- Enjoy eating what you have made!

FRENCH BREAD
PIZZA

French bread makes a great crust for pizza—thick and chewy. And this pizza is extra fun to eat because you get to choose the toppings! Have an adult assistant help with the cutting, slicing, and chopping and with the oven steps.

YOU NEED

INGREDIENTS

Favorite toppings, such as sliced pepperoni, sliced mushrooms, chopped green pepper, sliced zucchini, sliced tomatoes

1 loaf French or Italian bread

1 jar (14 or 15 ounces) pizza sauce

Oregano, to taste—about 1 teaspoon

1 package (12 ounces) shredded mozzarella cheese

KITCHEN TOOLS

2 cookie sheets • Aluminum foil • Sharp knife • Bread knife • Oven mitts • Spoon • Measuring spoons

1. Preheat the oven to 350°F. Cover the cookie sheets with aluminum foil.

2. Cut the bread in half lengthwise and then cut each half in thirds so that you have 6 pieces of bread. (If you like your pizza crisp, toast the bread first. Place it cut side up on the cookie sheets. Put on your oven mitts and place the cookie sheets in the oven for 2 or 3 minutes.)

3. Place the bread (toasted or not) on the cookie sheets, cut side up. Using a spoon, spread each piece with pizza sauce, dividing it evenly among the six pieces of bread. Sprinkle the sauce with oregano.

4. Sprinkle the toppings on the sauce. Top each pizza with 2 or 3 tablespoons of the shredded mozzarella cheese.

5. Wear oven mitts to place the cookie sheets in the oven. Bake until the cheese is bubbly, 10 to 12 minutes. With your oven mitts on, remove the cookie sheets from the oven.

Enjoy your pizza while it's hot!

MAKES 6 PIZZAS

QUESADILLAS

Mexican quesadillas (pronounced kay-sah DEE-yahs) are thin sandwiches made with refried beans and cheese on a tortilla—a flat, round Mexican bread. In a Mexican restaurant, quesadillas are often cut into triangles and served as an appetizer. You can serve them that way or keep them whole and serve them for lunch. Have an adult assistant help you with the oven steps.

YOU NEED

INGREDIENTS

6 tortillas (6- to 8-inch rounds)

1 can (15 ounces) refried beans

1 green bell pepper (optional)

1 package (8 ounces) shredded Monterey jack cheese

KITCHEN TOOLS

Cookie sheet • Aluminum foil • Sharp knife • Measuring spoons • Oven mitts

1. Preheat the oven to 350°F.

2. Wash the green pepper thoroughly, and stem, seed, and chop it.

3. Cover a cookie sheet with aluminum foil. Place the tortillas on the cookie sheet. Spread 2 tablespoons refried beans on each tortilla. Sprinkle with chopped green pepper, if you like. Then sprinkle each tortilla with 1 or 2 tablespoons shredded cheese.

4. Wear oven mitts to place the cookie sheet in the oven. Bake until the cheese is hot and bubbling, about 10 minutes. Wear oven mitts to take the cookie sheet out of the oven. Let the quesadillas cool until they're cool enough to eat, about 5 minutes.

MAKES 6 QUESADILLAS

POPOVERS

Popovers—fluffy, hollow muffins that are crusty on the outside and light on the inside—are called popovers because they do just that: As they bake, they pop up over the rim of the baking tin. Served right from the oven with butter or jam, or eaten just as they are, popovers make great breakfast treats. Have an adult assistant help with the oven steps.

YOU NEED

INGREDIENTS

2 tablespoons butter
    or margarine
2 eggs
1 cup milk
1 cup all-purpose flour
¼ teaspoon salt

KITCHEN TOOLS

Plastic sandwich bag • Two 6-cup muffin tins • Measuring cups • Measuring spoons • Large mixing bowl • Whisk • Oven mitts • Plate • Table knife

1. Preheat the oven to 375°F.

2. Place your hand in the sandwich bag and use it to generously grease the cups of the muffin tins with butter or margarine. Make sure to grease the rim of each cup.

3. Break the eggs into the mixing bowl and add the milk. Whisk until they are well blended.

4. Add the flour and salt and whisk them into the egg mixture.

5. With a ½-cup measuring cup, scoop out the batter and pour it into the muffin cups. Each should be one-half to two-thirds full.

6. Wear oven mitts to place the filled tin in the oven. Bake for 30 minutes without opening the oven door.

7. Wear oven mitts to take the muffin tins out of the oven. Turn them over so that the popovers fall out of the tin onto a plate. If any stick to the tins, use the table knife to loosen around the sides.
    Serve the popovers immediately!

MAKES 12 POPOVERS

TUNA FACES

A tuna sandwich is ordinary, but a tuna face is festive and appealing. When you have friends over for lunch, serve tuna face fixings and see who can make the funniest or most realistic face. You'll never look at tuna sandwiches the same way again!

Ask an adult assistant to help you slice the topping ingredients and manage the can opener.

YOU NEED

INGREDIENTS

Toppings such as pickle slices, shredded cheese, sprouts, scallions, (trimmed and cut lengthwise), red and green pepper strips, carrots cut into rounds, radish slices, olive slices, tomato wedges

2 cans (about 6 ounces each) tuna fish packed in water

Mayonnaise (to taste, about 2 tablespoons)

½ lemon, seeds removed

6 slices bread

KITCHEN TOOLS

Sharp knife • Small bowls for toppings • Can opener • Mixing bowl • Fork • Tablespoon • 6 plates • Large spoon

1. Put each topping in a small bowl, and place the bowls on the kitchen or dining-room table.

2. To make the tuna salad, open the cans of tuna and drain the liquid into the sink. Place the tuna in a mixing bowl and flake it with a fork into small pieces. Spoon in mayonnaise to taste, then squeeze in the juice from the lemon. If any lemon seeds happen to fall in, remove them. Use the fork to mix the tuna with the mayonnaise and lemon juice.

3. Place a slice of bread on each plate. Place a rounded scoop—use a large spoon—of tuna on each slice of bread and serve one to each person. Use the spoon to flatten the tuna into a circle.

4. Let everyone create a face using cheese, scallions, or sprouts for hair or whiskers; pickle slices for ears; radish, carrot, or olive slices for eyes; and red peppers or tomatoes for a mouth.

MAKES 6 FACES

QUICK TRICK

HOMEMADE SODA

Easy-to-make homemade soda has the fizz of store-bought soda, but it's not quite as sweet.

Fill a glass ⅔ full with your favorite fruit juice—orange, apple, or cranberry. Then add

INGREDIENTS
- Fruit juice
- Club soda

club soda and stir briefly. For variety, try mixing two or more fruit juices, like orange and cranberry or grape and lemonade, before adding the club soda.

YOGURT CHEESE

This creamy cheese made from yogurt is easy to make, but it does need time to set. Prepare the cheese first thing in the morning—or better yet, prepare it in the evening so that it can sit in the refrigerator overnight.

For a tasty snack, spread the cheese on crackers and top with a dollop of salsa. For a lunch treat, make the cheese with a flavored yogurt and then spread it on your favorite bread.

YOU NEED

INGREDIENTS

1 cup plain or flavored yogurt

KITCHEN TOOLS

Strainer • Large paper coffee filter • Bowl larger and deeper than the strainer • Tablespoon • Plastic wrap • Serving plate

1. Line the strainer with the coffee filter.

2. Place the strainer on top of the bowl. There should be space between the bottom of the bowl and the strainer. Spoon the yogurt into the coffee filter.

3. Cover the top of the bowl with plastic wrap. Place it in the refrigerator for at least 3 hours or overnight.

4. Remove the strainer from the bowl. Discard the liquid that has collected in the bowl. What remains in the coffee filter is yogurt cheese.

To serve, tip the cheese onto a plate. Enjoy yogurt cheese the way you would cream cheese.

MAKES ABOUT ⅔ CUP OF CHEESE

ZESTY TOASTED
CHEESE SANDWICHES

Chopped scallions add zest—and a bit of a surprise—to toasted cheese sandwiches. You can make them in the oven or, if you're making a small amount, in a toaster oven. Have an adult assistant help you slice the bread and scallions and help with the oven steps.

YOU NEED

INGREDIENTS

1 loaf Italian bread
2 scallions
6 ounces Cheddar or another hard cheese, sliced or shredded

KITCHEN TOOLS

Cookie sheet • Aluminum foil • Sharp knife • Measuring spoons • Oven mitts • Spatula • Serving plates

1. Preheat the oven to 350°F.

2. Cover the cookie sheet or the toaster oven tray with aluminum foil. Rinse the scallions under cold running water.

3. Slice the loaf of Italian bread into 10 or 12 rounds and thinly slice the green part of the scallions. (If you like, add the thinly sliced white part, too. It's sharper in taste.)

4. Place the bread rounds on the cookie sheet. Put about 1 teaspoon sliced scallions on the bread and top with cheese—either a slice cut to fit the bread or about 1 tablespoon shredded cheese.

5. Wear oven mitts to place the cookie sheet in the oven. Bake until the cheese is melted, about 5 minutes. Wear oven mitts to take the cookie sheet out of the oven. Use a spatula to put the toasted cheese sandwiches on plates. Serve right away.

MAKES 4 SERVINGS

MIXED GREEN SALAD
AND VINAIGRETTE

A salad of mixed greens with home-made dressing is easy to make. It's a great addition to any meal.

YOU NEED

INGREDIENTS

SALAD

1 small head red leaf lettuce

1 small bunch escarole

1 bunch watercress

8 to 12 cherry tomatoes

VINAIGRETTE

2 tablespoons olive oil

1 tablespoon balsamic or wine vinegar

1 teaspoon Dijon mustard

⅛ teaspoon each of 2 dried herbs, such as rosemary, tarragon, chives, or basil

Salt and pepper, to taste

KITCHEN TOOLS

Paper towels or salad spinner • Salad bowl and serving tools • Sharp knife • Measuring spoons • Small bowl, or a jar with a tight-fitting lid • Whisk, if needed

1. Separate lettuce and escarole leaves from core. Wash the lettuce, escarole, and watercress under cold running water. Dry the greens on paper towels or spin them dry in the salad spinner.

2. Tear the lettuce and escarole into bite-size pieces. Remove the stems from the watercress leaves and discard the stems. Place the greens in the salad bowl.

3. Wash and dry the tomatoes. Add them to the bowl.

4. Put all the vinaigrette ingredients into the small bowl (or jar; screw on the lid). Whisk or shake the jar until the ingredients are mixed.

Right before you plan to serve the salad, pour the dressing on the salad and toss it.

MAKES 6 SERVINGS

BAKED APPLES

Apples baking in the oven smell so good, you can hardly wait until they are done! But baked apples have to bake for about an hour, then have to cool for another half hour. Make them ahead of time if you want to serve them for lunch. Have an adult assistant help you core the apples and help with the oven steps.

YOU NEED

INGREDIENTS

6 medium baking apples
3 teaspoons sugar
½ teaspoon cinnamon
Raisins (optional)
1 cup water

KITCHEN TOOLS

Paper towels • Sharp knife or apple corer • Measuring spoons • Mixing spoon • Small bowl • Ovenproof baking dish • Measuring cup • Oven mitts • Fork

1. Preheat the oven to 350°F.

2. Rinse the apples thoroughly and dry them with paper towels. Core the apples, but leave the skin on.

3. Place the sugar and cinnamon in the small bowl and stir them together.

4. Place the apples in the baking dish right side up and carefully pour ½ teaspoon of the sugar and cinnamon mixture in the empty core of each one. Place some raisins in the core, too, if you like.

5. Measure the water and pour it into the pan around the bottom of the apples. Wear oven mitts to place the baking dish in the oven. Bake for 45 minutes to 1 hour, depending on the size of the apples. Wear oven mitts to test the apples with the fork. They are done when they are very soft but not too brown.

6. Wear oven mitts to take the baking pan out of the oven. Allow the apples to cool for at least 30 minutes before you eat them.

MAKES 6 SERVINGS

FRUIT KEBABS

Fruit kebabs—chunks of fruit on a wooden skewer—are an easy and pretty way to serve fruit for dessert. You can buy the skewers at a grocery or variety store. For an elegant touch, serve fruit kebabs with flavored yogurt— lemon or raspberry—for dipping.

Ask an adult assistant to help you peel and cut the fruit.

YOU NEED

INGREDIENTS

Fresh fruit, such as peaches, pears, nectarines, apples, bananas, melons, strawberries, large grapes

1 lemon or orange

1 cup flavored yogurt

KITCHEN TOOLS

Paper towels • Sharp knife • Cutting board • Wooden skewers (8 to 10 inches long) • Plates • Measuring spoons

1. Rinse the fruit thoroughly. Dry with paper towels.

2. On a cutting board, peel and cut the large fruit into large—at least 1-inch— chunks. Leave small fruit, like strawberries and grapes, whole.

3. Push the fruit onto the skewers, making sure each skewer has at least 1 chunk of each type of fruit. You'll want 5 or 6 pieces on each skewer.

4. Cut the lemon or orange in quarters and squeeze over the skewered fruit.

5. Put 1 or 2 skewers on each plate and add 2 tablespoons of yogurt.

SERVE AND ENJOY!

ORANGE CREAM
POPS

Cream pops are fun to make—just be sure to make them first thing in the morning so that they'll be ready for your afternoon snack. Create your own special flavors by making the pops with other flavors of juice—cranberry, grape, apple—and adding your favorite flavor of yogurt. Have an adult assistant help you with the knife step.

YOU NEED

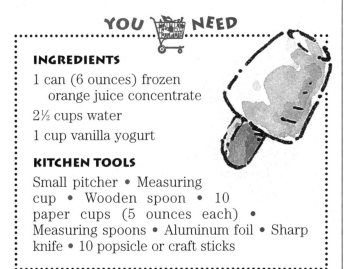

INGREDIENTS

1 can (6 ounces) frozen
   orange juice concentrate
2½ cups water
1 cup vanilla yogurt

KITCHEN TOOLS

Small pitcher • Measuring cup • Wooden spoon • 10 paper cups (5 ounces each) • Measuring spoons • Aluminum foil • Sharp knife • 10 popsicle or craft sticks

1. Let the frozen orange juice sit on a kitchen counter for 30 minutes to thaw slightly. Open it, and place the concentrate in a small pitcher. Measure the water and add it to the pitcher. Use the wooden spoon to mix the juice and water. If the concentrate is still frozen, the water should soften it up enough to mix after a few minutes.

2. Carefully pour the juice into the 10 paper cups, dividing it evenly.

3. Put 1 tablespoon yogurt into each cup, but do *not* stir.

4. Cover each cup with a small piece of aluminum foil. With a sharp knife, make a small slit in the center of the foil and put a popsicle stick through the foil so that it stands straight up in the cup.

5. Put the cups in the freezer for 3 hours or overnight. When you're ready to eat a pop, run hot water over the cup for a few seconds. The pop will pop right out.

MAKES 10 POPS

FROZEN BANANAS

For this yummy dessert or snack, you dip bananas in melted chocolate and then roll them in crushed dry cereal. For a treat that's less sweet, just roll the bananas in the crushed cereal (steps 1, 2, 3, and 6) and leaving out the chocolate (steps 4 and 5). Either way, frozen bananas are not to be missed. If you make them early in the day, they'll be ready for dessert at dinnertime. Ask an adult assistant to help you with the stovetop steps.

YOU NEED

INGREDIENTS
1 cup sweetened dry cereal
3 firm bananas
¾ cup semisweet chocolate chips

KITCHEN TOOLS
Small cookie sheet • Aluminum foil or waxed paper • Measuring cup • 1 plastic bag (1 gallon-size) with tie • Rolling pin (or large can or 1-liter bottle of soda) • Table knife • 6 popsicle or craft sticks • Double boiler • Pot holders • Wooden spoon

1. Cover the cookie sheet with aluminum foil or waxed paper.

2. Measure the cereal and put it into the plastic bag. Tie the bag to seal it. Crush the cereal with the rolling pin, large can, or soda bottle. Put the crushed cereal on a piece of waxed paper and set it aside.

3. Peel the bananas and cut them in half widthwise, not lengthwise. Insert a popsicle stick into the cut end of each banana. Set them aside on the cookie sheet.

4. Place some water in the bottom pot of a double boiler. Place the pot over medium heat. When the water comes to a simmer, lower the heat and keep the water at a simmer. Place the chocolate chips in the top of the double boiler. Use pot holders to carefully put the top pot over the pot with the simmering water. Melt the chips. When they are almost melted, use a wooden spoon to stir them around. Remember to hold the pots steady with a pot holder. (If you have a microwave oven, place the chips in a microwave-safe bowl, and put it, uncovered, in the microwave oven. Heat on high for 30 seconds, stir the chips, then microwave it, for another 10 to 15 seconds.)

5. As soon as the chips have melted, turn off the heat. Use pot holders to remove the top pot to a heatproof surface. Holding a banana by the stick, dip it into the chocolate. Use the wooden spoon to help cover the banana completely with the chocolate.

6. Roll the banana in the crushed cereal and put it on the cookie sheet. Repeat with the remaining bananas. Freeze for 3 hours or overnight.

MAKES 6 FROZEN BANANAS

QUICK TRICK

TRAIL MIX

Trail mix is easy to make with your favorite plain dry cereal and is a good snack to take along on a rainy-day indoor camping trip (page 4) as well as on hikes through the woods on sunny days.

INGREDIENTS
- 1 cup dry cereal
- ¼ cup raisins
- ¼ cup sunflower seeds
- ¼ cup nuts (optional)

■ Measure and gently mix together all the ingredients.

■ Divide the trail mix into the plastic bags, and secure the bags with twist ties.

MAKES 2 OR 3 SERVINGS

CHOCOLATE CHIP MUFFINS

Muffins are tasty treats, and they're simple to make. In this recipe, you add an extra ingredient you love—here it's chocolate chips, but you can use blueberries, strawberries, raisins, or apricots, instead—to a yellow cake mix. Ask an adult assistant to help you with the oven steps.

YOU  NEED

INGREDIENTS

2 tablespoons softened butter or margarine, if needed
1 box (18¼ ounces) yellow cake mix
1¼ cups water
⅓ cup vegetable oil
3 eggs
½ cup all-purpose flour
1 cup chocolate chips, or fresh blueberries or strawberries (chopped), or raisins, or dried apricots (chopped)

KITCHEN TOOLS

2 or more 6-cup muffin tins • Paper liners • Plastic sandwich bag, if needed • Large mixing bowl • Measuring cups • Electric mixer • Kitchen spoon • Oven mitts • Toothpick • Cooling rack

1. Preheat the oven 350°F.

2. Put the paper liners in the muffin tins. If you don't have paper liners, place your hand in the sandwich bag and use it to grease the tins with the butter or margarine. (If you don't have enough muffin tins to bake all the batter at once, bake the muffins in batches. Be sure to let the pans cool completely before starting the next batch.)

3. Place the cake mix in the mixing bowl. Add the water and oil, and then the eggs. Then add the flour. Using an electric mixer, stir the ingredients until blended. Stir in the chocolate chips or fruit with a spoon. Use the spoon to fill the cupcake liners about half full with the batter.

4. Wearing oven mitts, place the muffin tins in the oven and bake for 5 minutes longer than the time suggested for cupcakes on the cake mix box. To see if the muffins are done, insert a toothpick into the center of one muffin (wear oven mitts to do this). If it comes out clean, without any wet batter on it, the muffins are done.

5. Wearing oven mitts, remove the tins from the oven and place them on a heat-proof surface. Remove the muffins from the tins and cool on a rack for 15 minutes.

MAKES 24 MUFFINS

LEMON DROP
COOKIES

Tart, lemony cookies are easy to make when you start with cake mix. For variety, try making cookies from other cake mixes, like banana, chocolate, or carrot. Have an adult assistant help with the oven steps.

YOU NEED

INGREDIENTS
1 box (18¼ ounces) lemon cake mix
⅓ cup vegetable oil
2 eggs
½ cup raisins (optional)

KITCHEN TOOLS
Large mixing bowl • Measuring cup • Measuring spoons • Electric mixer • Cookie sheets • Oven mitts • Metal spatula • Cooling rack or plate

1. Preheat the oven to 350°F.

2. Place the cake mix in the bowl. Add the oil and the eggs to the bowl. Using an electric mixer, mix the ingredients together. The cookie dough will be stiff. If you like, add raisins to the mixture and mix until they are blended in.

3. Drop the dough by tablespoon onto ungreased cookie sheets. The cookies should be about 2 inches apart.

4. Wearing oven mitts, place the cookie sheets in the oven. Bake the cookies for 11 minutes, then check to see if they're done. The cookies will have spread and will look firm. If they're not done yet, let them bake another 2 minutes and check again.

5. Wearing oven mitts, take the cookies out of the oven and place the cookie sheets on a heatproof surface. Let the cookies cool about 10 minutes. Then, using the spatula, move the cookies to a rack or a plate to cool completely.

MAKES ABOUT 36 COOKIES

BANANA
SMOOTHIE

A velvety-smooth drink made with yogurt, fruit, and fruit juice—what could be better! Use any fruit that's in season (or drained canned fruit), or try a combination of several fruits to create your own distinctive drink.

Ask an adult assistant to help you with cutting up the fruit, opening the cans, and running the blender.

YOU  NEED

INGREDIENTS

1 ripe banana
½ cup chopped fresh fruit (not banana) or drained canned fruit
1 cup flavored yogurt
½ cup fruit juice
Dash of nutmeg

KITCHEN TOOLS

Sharp knife • Can opener, if needed • Strainer, if needed • Measuring cup • Blender • 2 tall glasses

1. Cut the banana into chunks. If the other fruit you chose is large, such as a peach, pear, or pineapple, peel it, and cut it into chunks. Small fruit, like strawberries or blueberries, can go into the blender whole. If you are using canned fruit, open the cans and pour the fruit into a strainer to drain the liquid.

2. Measure the fruit, yogurt, and juice and place in the blender. Place the lid on the blender and blend for just 5 seconds. Turn off the blender and check the mixture. If there are still chunks, put the lid back on and blend for another 5 seconds.

3. Divide the smoothies evenly between 2 glasses and top with a dash of nutmeg.

MAKES 2 LARGE SMOOTHIES

CHOCOLATE
CRUNCH BARS

For these sweet, crunchy snack bars, you can use 1 cup each of four different dry cereals, 2 cups of two different cereals, or add the last bit of the cereal at the bottom of several boxes to one of your favorites: Cheerios, corn flakes, Rice Krispies, or flakes with raisins and nuts.

Ask an adult assistant to help with the stovetop steps and cutting the bars.

YOU NEED

INGREDIENTS

3 tablespoons of margarine, plus 1 teaspoon softened margarine for greasing the pan

4 cups dry cereal

2 cups mini or regular marshmallows (about 6 ounces)

1 cup chocolate chips

KITCHEN TOOLS

Plastic sandwich bag • 12- by 7-inch baking pan • Large mixing bowl • Measuring cup • Double boiler • Pot holders • Wooden spoon • Kitchen spoon • Sharp knife

1. Place your hand in the sandwich bag and use it to spread 1 teaspoon of margarine on the bottom and sides of the baking pan.

2. Measure out the different kinds of cereal and use your hand to mix them together in a mixing bowl.

3. Place some water in the bottom pot of a double boiler. Place the pot over medium heat until the water comes to a simmer. Lower the heat to keep the water at a simmer. Measure the marshmallows and chocolate chips. Place them in the top of the double boiler with 3 tablespoons of margarine. Using pot holders, put the top pot over the pot with the simmering water. Melt the ingredients, stirring occasionally. (If you have a microwave oven, place the ingredients in a microwave-safe bowl and place it, uncovered, in the microwave oven on high for 30 seconds. Stir, then microwave for another 10 to 15 seconds.)

4. When the chocolate mixture is melted, turn off the heat. Using pot holders, remove the top pot from the bottom one and pour the chocolate mixture onto the cereal. Use a wooden spoon to stir the mixture until the cereal is coated with the chocolate.

5. Press the mixture into the baking pan and refrigerate for 1 hour. When the mixture is set, ask an adult to use a sharp knife to cut it into 16 pieces.

MAKES 16 BARS

BANANA S'MORES

Not only is this scrumptious dessert quick to make, but it's easy to eat. The banana skin becomes the bowl you serve it in! Ask an adult assistant for help with slitting the banana skins and with the oven steps.

YOU NEED

INGREDIENTS

6 bananas

6 tablespoons semisweet chocolate chips

1 cup miniature marshmallows

KITCHEN TOOLS

Sharp knife • Measuring spoons • Measuring cup • Aluminum foil • Cookie sheet • Oven mitts

1. Preheat the oven to 400°F.

2. Slit each banana skin on the inside curve with a sharp knife, taking care not to cut the banana. Use your hands to loosen the skin slightly, but keep the ends together.

3. For each banana, tuck 1 tablespoon of chips and some of the marshmallows along the sides of each banana between the fruit and the skin. Push the skin together—it won't close completely—and wrap the banana tightly in aluminum foil. Place the foil-wrapped bananas on a cookie sheet.

4. Wearing oven mitts, place the cookie sheet in the oven. Bake the bananas for 10 minutes.

5. Wear oven mitts to take the cookie sheet out of the oven. Let the bananas cool for a few minutes. Open the foil, carefully so that you aren't surprised by a hot burst of steam.

Eat the bananas and the melted chocolate-marshmallow sauce right out of the skin with a spoon.

MAKES 6 S'MORES

ICE CREAM
SANDWICHES

Ice cream sandwiches are a treat any day, rainy or full of sunshine! You can choose your favorite flavor of ice cream and pair it with your favorite cookies. Try combinations like vanilla ice cream and chocolate cookies, caramel ice cream on peanut butter cookies edged with chopped nuts, strawberry ice cream on oatmeal cookies rolled in cookie crumbs, or orange sherbet on lemon cookies dipped in toasted coconut.

YOU 🛒 NEED

INGREDIENTS
1 pint ice cream
12 large or 20 small cookies
Sprinkles

KITCHEN TOOLS
Waxed paper or plastic bags • Tablespoon • Large spoon or ice cream scoop

1. Remove the ice cream from the freezer, and put it the refrigerator for about 10 minutes, until it softens slightly.

2. While the ice cream softens, put the sprinkles on a piece of waxed paper.

3. Remove the ice cream from the refrigerator. Place a large scoop of ice cream on top of 6 large cookies (or put a small scoop on top of 10 smaller cookies). Then press another cookie on top.

4. With a tablespoon, smooth the sides of the ice cream sandwich. Then roll the sides in sprinkles. Serve right away, or wrap the sandwiches individually in waxed paper or plastic bags and place them in the freezer until you're ready to serve them.

MAKES 6 TO 10 SANDWICHES

GUMMY RAINDROPS

What could be better on a rainy day than candy raindrops? They take only a few minutes to make, and you get to choose the flavors. They're not as sweet as store-bought candy, so it's okay to eat a whole handful!

For more intense flavor, add 1 or 2 drops of liquid flavorings—such as almond, peppermint, or vanilla—to the boiled juice. Ask an adult assistant for help with the stovetop steps.

YOU NEED

INGREDIENTS
¼ cup cranberry, apple, or grape juice
1 envelope unflavored gelatin
1 tablespoon sugar

KITCHEN TOOLS
Measuring cup • Small saucepan • Pot holders • Wooden spoon • Cookie sheets • Waxed paper • Measuring spoons

1. Measure the fruit juice and place it in a small saucepan. Heat the fruit juice over medium heat until it boils. Turn off the heat and, using pot holders, remove the pan from the heat.

2. Immediately sprinkle the gelatin on top of the fruit juice. Using pot holders to hold the pot, stir the mixture with a wooden spoon until the gelatin dissolves.

3. Cover the cookie sheet with waxed paper. Then spoon the gelatin mixture onto the cookie sheet in 1-inch raindrops. Allow them to cool slightly, then sprinkle lightly with sugar.

Cool on the cookie sheet for 10 more minutes, then peel the raindrops from the waxed paper.

MAKES ABOUT 36 CANDIES

CREATIVE
THINKING

Between school, sports, and family activities, there's seldom time to let your imagination run wild. Writing poetry, telling stories, even designing fantasy rooms for your home are all ways to stretch your mind and have fun at the same time. And once your creative juices really start flowing, you may never want to stop. Whether you spend 10 minutes brainstorming or 10 years keeping a journal, you'll find that these activities will lead you to a new way of looking at yourself and the world.

YOUR OWN CARTOON STRIPS

Create comic strips starring your family and friends.

> Photographs or pictures cut from magazines • White paper • Pen or pencil • Scissors • Construction paper • Felt-tipped markers • Glue

1. Look through your spare family photographs—those that are not framed or in a photo album, and that no one's saving. Choose three or four of them, some of people in a group and some of one person alone. If you don't have extra family photographs, you can cut out photographs of people from old magazines.

2. Think of things for the people to say: funny sayings for individual photographs or humorous dialogues for group photographs. If you have enough photos that relate to each other, you can create a series of boxes like in a comic strip.

3. When you have thought of the sayings, write them on a piece of white paper. Cut around them in the shape of a cartoon speech balloon.

4. Glue the photographs in the order you want to a piece of construction paper. Then glue the speech balloons above and pointing to the people's heads. With a marker, draw a line around each balloon.

For extra fun, make collages of family photos and magazine ads. Put your mother's face on a baby's body or your baby brother's head on a bodybuilder's torso—and then think of things for them to say.

CREATE A STORY

This is a great activity for five or six players, but it also works for two.

Paper and pencils

1. Give a piece of paper and a pencil to every player. Everyone starts a story by writing one or two sentences and begins another sentence.

Here's an opening to get you started: *It was a dark and stormy night. The rain was coming down in torrents. Suddenly, Jared heard the crash of . . .* Or try this one: *The sun was beating down. It was Jessica's turn at bat. The ball came straight at her. She swung hard and . . .*

2. When all the players have finished their introductions, everyone passes his paper to the right. Each player finishes the incomplete sentence, writes another sentence or two, and begins a new sentence on the new page. Then everyone passes his paper to the right again.

3. Each player finishes the previous player's sentence and writes one or two new ones, leaving a sentence unfinished for the next player to complete.

If only two or three people are playing, you can pass the papers around twice. Decide ahead of time how many passes to allow to complete the story.

4. Read the completed stories aloud.

WRITE AND ILLUSTRATE
A BOOK

Write and illustrate a picture book about your own experience or one in your imagination. Here are some ideas to get you started.

YOU NEED

Paper • Pencil or pen • Drawings or photographs • Construction paper • White glue • Hole punch • Brass paper fasteners

■ Find some old photographs of a family trip or holiday gathering. It's more fun to use ones in which everybody doesn't look perfect. Mom's eyes are closed; Dad's got food on his face—you get the idea. Make up a story about what's going on and illustrate it with the photographs.

■ If you have a pet, write a collection of stories about the mischief your pet gets into. Draw pictures or take photographs of your pet.

■ You can write scary stories or science fiction or stories about a favorite action figure or stories from a doll's point of view.

■ If you have a favorite hobby like baseball, stamp collecting, or bird watching, write and illustrate an informative guide to the hobby. If you live in a town with interesting monuments, museums, and parks, write an illustrated tour guidebook.

■ It's easier to begin writing a story if you first make a list of things about your subject. For example, list the landmarks in your neighborhood or the tricks your pet can perform. Each idea can become a page or chapter in your book.

■ When you're happy with your list, write about each item. If you're making the illustrations, create a drawing for each idea. If you're using photographs, match the pictures to the writing. If you like, revise and rewrite until you really like the way the story sounds.

■ To make the book, arrange the written portions and the drawings or photographs on construction paper. When you are pleased with the arrangement, glue everything to the construction paper. Make a cover with another piece of construction paper.

■ Make a neat pile of all the construction paper pages and punch two holes on the left side with a hole punch. Put a brass paper fastener through each hole and bend the ends to hold the book together.

FIDO
THE
SUPER
DOG

MR. FIDO

HAIKU AND CINQUAIN

Short poems may look simple, but they are very often challenging to write. The challenge is in saying something in a very few words—just the right words, of course. Sometimes the very tightness of the structure helps the writer.

■ Try your hand at writing haiku (pronounced HIGH-koo). Haiku is a Japanese style of poem that has three lines. The first line has five syllables, the second line seven, and the last line five. (A syllable is a word or a part of a word that is spoken with a single sound. The word *heart* has one syllable, *hearty* has two, and *heartily* has three syllables.)

Here's an example of a haiku to help you get started:

The day is cold and
1 2 3 4 5

She feels lonely by the fire.
1 2 3 4 5 6 7

Then she thinks of you.
1 2 3 4 5

■ You also might like to try writing a cinquain (pronounced SING-cane). A cinquain is a five-line poem; its name comes from *cinq*, the French word for five. The first line of the poem has one word; the second line two words; the third line three words; the fourth line four words; and the fifth line has one word. Here's a cinquain:

Monkey—
Squeaking animal
Climbing on bars,
Eating bananas when hungry,
Happy.

A haiku often expresses a mood or place, while a cinquain is usually more descriptive or portrait-like. Try writing a haiku about a hot summer day, or a cinquain about your favorite cat or dog.

BRAINSTORM

Brainstorming is a way of tossing ideas around to come up with the solution to a problem, to develop a clever idea, or just to think about something silly or whimsical. Sometimes thoughts trickle in like a light sprinkling of rain; other times the thoughts pour in so fast that you have to write like the wind to get them all down on paper. The game of brainstorming is simple to play, but it keeps your brain cells active. You can play alone or with friends.

YOU ✂ NEED

Paper and pencils • Clock with a second hand or a kitchen timer

■ First make a list of things to name or describe. For instance, think of five ways to cure hiccups, twelve Christmas stocking stuffers, seven considerate things to do for your sister or brother, eight ways to make new friends, ten countries you would like to visit, or six foods you would never eat.

■ If you are playing with a friend or friends, time your game. Read out one of the categories on your list, and give all players 2 minutes to write down as many items as they can. At the end, read your lists aloud. Expect some pretty funny answers!

KEEP A JOURNAL

A slow Saturday afternoon is a great time to think about your life and write down your thoughts down in a journal. Not only is it a good way to practice writing, but keeping a journal will probably help you get to know yourself a bit better.

If you write about your life, school, friends, and family in a journal, you can keep it private and not show it to anyone, or you can share it, if and when you like.

YOU NEED

Spiral notebook or composition book • Pencil

■ Use a spiral notebook or composition book and write about who you are, who you live with, what you do, what you think and wonder about, and how you feel. Some ideas to start you off:

- How old are you?
- Does your younger brother or sister embarrass or enchant you?
- Do you look up to or avoid your older sister or brother?
- How do you feel about your family?
- What's your ideal pet?
- What would you like your room to look like?
- What's the naughtiest thing you have ever done?
- What are you proudest of?
- If you were going to start a collection, what would you collect?
- What's the worst movie you ever saw?
- What's the best book you ever read?
- Are there more books by the same author that you would like to read?
- If you could take a trip anywhere, where would you go? Why? How would you get there?
- What's the silliest thing your parents ever did?
- What are the three things that worry you the most?
- Which three things make you feel the happiest?
- What are you learning in school?
- What do you and your friends like to do for fun?

- What's the best show on television?
- Would you like to be in that show?
- What's your favorite sport?
- What is the best thing a teacher ever did in class?
- What are the two most wonderful things about your life?

■ Try to write in your journal at least once a week. *Never* throw out your journal. Not only is it fun to read while you are writing it, it will be even more fun to read several years from now.

BE A PEN PAL

It's thought-provoking (and may even be comforting) to think of all the people in the world as your extended family.

If you would like to find a pen pal, ask people you know if they have friends or relatives in another part of the world. Or write to one of the organizations in the box on the facing page.

YOU  NEED

Paper and pencil

■ Someone who lives a different life than you do is likely to be as curious about you as you are about them. Imagine the questions your pen pal might ask. Here are some examples.

- How old are you?
- Where do you go to school?
- What is your house like?
- Who is in your family?
- What are your favorite toys and games?
- Do you like sports?

- What kinds of foods do you eat?
- What are your favorite books?
- What do you do in your free time?
- Who is your best friend and why?
- How do you celebrate your favorite holiday?

Then, try answering these questions in your letter. Your letter will definitely be interesting to a pen pal. It may even be the beginning of a lifelong friendship.

WHERE TO FIND A PEN PAL

Write away right away!

The organizations listed below are for people who want to write to people around the world or in the United States. They match correspondents by age, sex, and language. With some, you can ask for a pen pal in a particular state or country, while others simply assign you a pen pal. For information, send your name, address, and age and include a stamped, self-addressed envelope. Some of these organizations charge a small fee; others are free.

American Kids Pen Pal Club
P.O. Box 2
Elizabeth, AR 72531

Friends Around the World
P.O. Box 10266
Merrillville, IN 46411

International Pen Friends
P.O. Box 290065
Brooklyn, NY 11229

World Pen Pals
1694 Como Avenue
St. Paul, MN 55708

Worldwide Friendship International
3749 Brice Run Road, Suite A
Randallstown, MD 21133

TAKE A TRIP
TO MARS . . . BACK IN HISTORY . . .

You don't need a spaceship or a time machine to get you out of the house—*way* out of the house. All you need is your imagination . . .

YOU ❖ NEED

> Paper and pencil

■ Imagine what it would be like to travel to Mars. You'd have plenty of food in your trusty spaceship. What other things would you want to bring along? Pack a bag with the items you would most want to take with you. Why did you choose them?

■ Head back in time to meet up with the most fascinating people in history? Who would you like to meet? King Arthur? Cleopatra? Thomas Jefferson? What about your own great-great-grandmother or the person who invented the wheel? What would you want to know about the person's life? Think about the questions you would want to ask him or her.

■ You're a scientist working in a high-tech laboratory. Is there one invention that would make your life easier? How about a machine that gets you dressed in the morning while you're still sleeping? Or a skateboard-mobile that gets you to school or your friend's house as fast as an airplane? Invent a machine that would change the way you do things. Draw a picture of it, and then explain how it works.

BE AN
INTERIOR DESIGNER

Design the bedroom, playroom, or fantasy game room you have always wanted, and then build it—with paper.

Graph paper • Pencil • Construction paper • Carton • Scissors or craft knife • Gift wrap or contact paper • Felt-tipped markers • Poster paint and brushes • White glue • Fabric scraps • Small boxes • Craft sticks

1. Start by making a floor plan. Draw the shape of your fantasy room on graph paper, making 1 inch (four squares) equal to 1 foot. Then draw the door, windows and closets.

2. Decide what pieces of furniture you want in your room. Make small furniture shapes to scale (again, 1 inch to 1 foot) out of colored construction paper or graph paper that you have colored with markers. (Measure your own furniture to get common sizes of chairs, tables, and beds.)

Make a pleasing arrangement of furniture, and then add special touches like a stereo, a television set, or potted plants and trees. These, too, can be made from construction paper.

3. To make a three-dimensional room, find a cardboard carton or large box. Cut off one side to make an open front. Trim the box to the size of your floor plan. If one side is too long, cut it off (ask an adult assistant for help with this), shorten the bottom of the box (the floor), and tape the side back on. Cut out the door and windows, and draw in the closet doors.

4. Glue gift wrap or contact paper to the walls to create wallpaper, or create your own wall covering with markers or paint.

5. For furniture, use cardboard, craft sticks, and odds and ends.

• To make a four-poster bed, tape drinking straws cut in half to a small gift box. You can even glue lace trim to the tops of the straws for a canopy.

- For a bureau, stand a rectangular box upright and draw in the drawers.
- For a table, cut out a circle of cardboard and glue it to an empty thread spool.
- To make chairs, turn a small square box upside down and glue two craft sticks upright to the back. For the chair-back rungs, glue toothpicks between the craft sticks.

- To make an easy chair, turn a small square box upside down and glue the cover to one side so that it stands upright.
- Make a bedspread from fabric cut from an old shirt, a rug from a piece of an old sweatshirt. You can even add curtains by gluing fabric to the windows.

READY
TO WEAR

With a little imagination you can transform every-day objects into wearable works of art. Why not give an old stained T-shirt new life? Or turn a basic barrette into a thing of beauty? You'll look great wearing a money pouch you made or carrying a customized lunch bag. And every time you look at your clothes and accessories, you'll remember the fun you had making them. What's more, they'll probably make you want to show off a little—since you were the chief designer.

SPECIAL T

Don't let a stain ruin a favorite T-shirt (or sweatshirt). Here's a way to cover it up and create a new shirt at the same time. Make sure the shirt is clean and dry before you start.

YOU ✂ NEED

Old T-shirt • Fabric scraps • Scissors • Newspaper • Cardboard • Fabric paint • Other decorations (optional)

1. Cut fabric scraps into circles, squares, triangles, stars, hearts, or other shapes, about 2 to 3 inches in size. Then, cover a table with newspaper and lay the shirt flat. Slip a piece of cardboard between the front and back of the shirt to protect it and to give you a firm work surface.

2. Arrange your fabric shapes on the shirt in a design that is pleasing to you. It could be a flower, with each petal a separate fabric piece, or a solar system, or an abstract arrangement. Move the shapes around until you're happy with the design.

3. Glue each fabric shape to the T-shirt with fabric paint, applying the fabric paint to your cutouts in a line wide enough to cover both the edge of the fabric piece and some of the T-shirt. (Fabric paint is available at variety and art supply stores.) The fabric paint will act as glue, attaching the fabric shapes to the shirt. Make sure all the cut edges of your shapes are edged in paint, or the shapes will fray when your shirt is washed.

Add ribbons, fancy buttons, large sequins, or other decorations, if you like, by gluing them in place with fabric paint. Let the paint dry overnight.

PERSONALIZED
LUNCH BAGS

Personalize ordinary brown paper lunch bags with your name or initials and a design. These bags usually come in packages of 50 and are quick to decorate. A snappy design is sure to look sharp in the cafeteria, and may even make that tuna sandwich taste better.

YOU NEED

New sponge • Scissors • Newspaper • Brown paper lunch bags • Poster paint • Pie plate or shallow bowl

■ On a new sponge, print your name or initials in block letters. Then draw small shapes for decoration: circles (trace around a bottle cap), squares, triangles, and curves. With scissors, cut the letters and shapes out.

■ Now, cover your work area with newspaper. Pour some paint into a pie plate or shallow bowl. Dampen your sponge shapes with water and squeeze out excess. Dip a sponge shape lightly into the paint and press it onto the paper bag. Continue dipping and pressing the shapes to get your initials and the design you want.

■ When it's complete, put the bag on newspaper until it's dry.

You can make enough bags—with different designs—to last for at least a week's worth of lunches.

MONEY POUCH

eed a place to keep money that you take to school or to the store? This simple money pouch slips onto your belt.

1. Measure, mark, and cut a piece of felt 4 by 12 inches. On one side of the felt (what will be the inside of the money pouch), draw the fold lines, slit lines, and marks for the holes as follows.

- With the piece of felt lengthwise, mark the fold lines, with a pencil. Make one line 4 inches up from the bottom edge and make another line 4 inches down from the top edge.
- For the slit lines in the middle section, make two 2-inch-long lines starting 1 inch up from the fold line and 1 inch in from the outside edges.
- To mark the place for each hole, starting ½ inch up from the bottom and ½

inch in from the outside edges, make a dot every ¾ inch on the right and left edges of the bottom section. Then, starting ½ inch up from the fold line, do the same in the middle section.

2. With scissors, round the top corners. Then fold the felt in half so that half of each slit line is visible and cut each slit (b). Open the felt. With a hole punch, make a hole at each dot along both sides.

3. Sew a button onto the front section. (It's easier to sew the button on when the pouch is still flat, so don't wait until after the pouch is finished.) To mark the spot for the button, turn the felt to what will be the outside (the side without the pencil markings). Pencil a dot 2 inches down from the end *without* the rounded

144

corners and 2 inches in from the sides.

Thread a needle with a double length of thread and make a knot at the end. Sew the button on top of the pencil dot.

4. Fold the pouch along the bottom fold line with the pencil lines on the inside and the holes aligned. Use about 18 inches of lanyard to lace the bottom and middle sections together as follows: Leaving a 2- or 3-inch tail, thread the lanyard through the holes on one side of the pouch from back to front. Bring the lanyard around the edge of the felt and thread it into the next hole from the back (c). Continue lacing this way. At the top, cut off the excess lanyard, leaving a 2-inch tail.

To secure the beginning and end tails of lanyard, thread them through the stitches at the back of the pouch. Lace the other side the same way.

5. To make the buttonhole, fold the top flap down so that it covers the button. Feel for the button underneath and make a short horizontal line that's just slightly larger than the button on the flap. Open the flap, fold it in half vertically, and carefully cut a buttonhole in the felt the same way you cut the belt slits.

To wear the pouch, slip your belt through the two slits in the back.

DOUGH MONSTER
CHAIN

Make a real cookie monster head and big, chunky beads with homemade dough.

Modeling dough (see Project) • Waxed paper • Straw or chopstick • Poster paint • Brushes • Leather thong or shoelace

1. Put your dough on a piece of waxed paper, and pound and knead it like bread dough to get rid of air bubbles.

2. Take a large piece of the dough to mold your monster's head and smaller pieces to make large, chunky beads.

3. Use a straw or a chopstick to make a hole through the top of your monster head and through the center of each bead. Let them dry on waxed paper overnight.

4. The next day, paint the beads with poster paint and put them on waxed paper to dry. When they're dry, thread them onto a leather thong or a colorful shoelace.

HOMEMADE DOUGH

Mix, knead, sculpt!

INGREDIENTS

1 cup cornstarch
2 cups baking soda
1¼ cups cold water

KITCHEN TOOLS

Saucepan • Measuring cups • Pot holder • Wooden spoon • Bowl • Damp cloth

1. Mix the cornstarch and the baking soda in a saucepan. Then add the water and stir with a wooden spoon until the mixture is smooth.

2. Hold the pot with a pot holder and cook over medium heat for a few minutes until the mixture looks like mashed potatoes. Ask an adult assistant for help with this step.

3. Spoon the dough into a bowl. Cover with a damp cloth until the dough is cool enough to handle, about 30 minutes.

MAGAZINE BEADS

Take recycling to new—and glamorous—lengths! Make striking beads from magazine photos or ads.

YOU NEED

Magazine pages • Scissors • Ruler • Toothpicks • White glue • Dental floss • Construction paper (optional) • Empty 15-ounce can (optional)

1. Choose an old magazine that nobody's saving, and from the brightest pages, cut rectangles and triangles that are 1 to 2 inches wide and 2 to 4 inches long.

The size and shape of the paper you cut will determine the size and shape of the bead you make. A rectangle becomes a bead shaped like a tube; the wider the rectangle, the longer the bead. A triangle becomes a lozenge-shaped bead. The longer the triangle, the thicker the center of the bead.

2. To make the beads, lay the paper shapes on the table with the colorful side face down. Put a toothpick at one short end of a rectangle or at the base of a triangle and roll the paper up around the toothpick. Put glue on the end of the paper to keep the bead rolled up. Remove the toothpick. Repeat for as many beads as you want.

3. When the glue is dry, thread the beads onto a piece of dental floss. You can combine these beads with beads you purchase at a craft store or old buttons to make an interesting necklace.

Since these beads are relatively flat, you can use them to make a mosaic picture. Sort your beads into color groups, then place them on a piece of construction paper to make a design. When you are pleased with the design, use white glue to secure each bead.

To make a handsome pencil holder, glue beads to a clean, empty, 15-ounce can.

PONYTAIL HOLDER

Dress up a terry cloth ponytail holder with buttons and beads in colors to match your clothes.

YOU NEED

Large button • Ruler • Narrow ribbon • Scissors • Small beads • Terry-cloth ponytail holder • Needle • Thread

1. Scavenge or buy a large button with four holes. Measure and cut 1 yard of ⅛- or ¹⁄₁₆-inch wide ribbon into four equal 9-inch pieces. (The width of the ribbon depends on the size of the holes in the button.)

2. Working from the front of the button, thread one end of one piece of ribbon through any hole and the other end through the opposite hole. Both ends of the ribbon are now at the back of the button. Pull the ends to make them even. Repeat with a second piece of ribbon in the same holes (a).

3. Holding one end of the pair of ribbons tight against one hole, thread the other end through that hole to the front (b). Bring the other end of the pair up through the opposite hole. You should now have four ribbon ends, two from each of two opposite holes, coming out of the front of the button (c).

4. Repeat these steps with the other two ribbons and the other two diagonally opposite holes in the button. You should now have eight ribbon ends coming out of the four holes in the front of the button.

5. Thread through each ribbon end a small (6-millimeter) bead, and tie a knot at the end of each ribbon to keep the bead from slipping off.

You can use beads of the same color or use different colors. You can also use more than one bead on a ribbon, or you can mix beads, bells, seashells, and other decorations.

6. With a needle and double sewing thread, attach the decorated button to a terry-cloth ponytail holder. Sew through the layers of ribbon on the back of the button, and then wrap the thread around the ponytail holder. Repeat several times to secure the button to the ponytail holder.

QUICK ⏱ TRICK

RIBBON-COVERED HEADBAND

Don't throw out that worn-out fabric head-band. Recycle it to match a new outfit instead. You'll need a ribbon about 1 inch wide and 1¼ yards long.

■ To cover the headband, turn under ½ inch of the ribbon at one cut end, put white glue on it, and hold it on the inside of one end of the headband. With your other hand, start wrapping the ribbon around the headband, holding the ribbon at a slight diagonal and making sure each wrap over-laps the previous one.

YOU NEED
- Headband
- Ribbon
- Scissors
- White glue

■ At the other end of the headband, trim away any excess ribbon and fold under ½ inch. Glue this folded end on the inside. Allow the glue to dry before putting on your headband.

■ To add a bow, follow the directions for the bow barrette on page 150. Tie the bow around the headband about 2 inches from the center.

BOW BARRETTE

Wearing hair bows is fun but somehow, the bows never manage to stay tied! You can tie bows on barrettes that will stay put all day. Make two small barrettes or one big one to wear at the back.

YOU ✂ NEED

1 yard of 1-inch wide ribbon • Ruler • Scissors • Barrette backings • White glue

■ For a small barrette, measure and cut two pieces of ribbon, each 9 inches long. With one piece of ribbon, make a loop, overlapping the cut ends. Place the loop on top of the barrette backing (available at craft stores) with the cut ends on the backing (a).

Slip one end of the other piece of ribbon under the top bar of the barrette in the center of the loop and tie the ribbon in a knot (b). Twist the knot so that it is at the back of the barrette. Pull the ribbon ends down to make them look nice (c). Trim the ends diagonally, if you like. Put a drop or two of white glue on the knot to keep it secure.

■ Follow the same steps to make a matching small barrette. Be sure to let the barrettes dry before you use them.

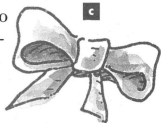

■ For a large barrette, measure and cut a piece of ribbon at least 12 inches long, so that when the ribbon is doubled the loop will cover the barrette.

Then measure and cut a second loop of ribbon 9 inches long and place it on top of the first one. Use the remaining ribbon to tie the loops and barrette together in the center, as described above.

SAFETY PIN
BRACELET

Safety pins are not only useful, but they can be used to make a colorful and stylish bangle bracelet. You can use brass pins or silver pins or a combination of both (as long as they're the same size). And you can experiment with beads of the same color on each safety pin, or you can mix up the colors. A 6-inch bracelet takes 32 size 0 (⅞-inch) safety pins and a package of 4-millimeter beads. Adjust quantities for a larger or smaller bracelet.

YOU ✄ NEED

Small safety pins • Tiny beads

1. To begin, put three beads—of the same color, if you want to create a pattern with the color—on a safety pin and close it. Make 24 of these beaded pins.

2. Arrange the pins in eight groups of three, with the head of each pin—the part you open and close—on the right. (The bracelet looks best if all the pins face the same direction.) When you have arranged the colors the way you want, align all the safety pins so that the arm without the beads is on top.

3. When you connect the groups of pins, you will be working on what will be the back of the bracelet. To connect each group of three safety pins to the group next to it, first open one of your empty pins. Alternating between the two groups, pick up the tail of one pin, then the head of the next pin until both sets (all six safety pins) are connected. Add another group of three pins to these two groups the same way. Continue adding groups until all eight groups are attached.

4. Before you attach the last safety pin—the one that connects the last group of three pins to the first group, making a circle—measure the bracelet on your wrist. If it slips on easily, then attach the last safety pin. If you need more length, add another link—another group of three safety pins with beads.

MAGIC
TRICKS

Knots that magically untie. Balloons that won't pop. Faces that disappear before your eyes. It's magic! And you can perform it. Pulling off tricks or stunts, making predictions, reading minds, and doing the (seemingly) impossible will amaze your friends.

The tricks in this chapter don't require any special equipment, just things you have around the house, like a deck of cards, string or rope, and paper and scissors.

Magic is fun, and rainy days and Saturdays are good times to learn some new tricks.

TIPS FROM
MONDO THE MAGNIFICENT

If you plan to put on a show, it helps to rehearse some patter, a magician's word for what you say to the audience as you perform the tricks. Patter keeps up the suspense and can distract audience members so that they don't pay close attention to what you are doing.

It's also great to have your own magic word to use instead of "abracadabra." You could make up a word of your own or use a silly phrase like "Fried bananas!"

Most magic tricks depend on sleight of hand, which means being quick and skillful with your hands, so quick that you fool the audience. So, before you put on a show, figure out which tricks you want to present and practice, practice, practice!

CHAINED!

Make three paper clips link them selves together like loops in a chain without touching the clips. Here's how.

YOU ❖ NEED

$1 bill • Paper clips

■ Fold a $1 bill in half lengthwise. Then fold it into thirds, folding the right third toward the back and the left third toward the front. From the side, the dollar bill will look like a Z (a).

■ Put one paper clip at the left, clipping the back and middle sections only. Put the next paper clip in the center, clipping together the center and front sections. Put the last one on the right, also clipping together the center and front sections (b).

■ Hold an end of the dollar in each hand and say a magic word as you quickly pull on both ends of the bill. The dollar will straighten out and send a chain of paper clips flying through the air.

GEORGE FLIPS!

You can make George Washington flip for you. Well, at least stand on his head. Here's how.

$1 bill

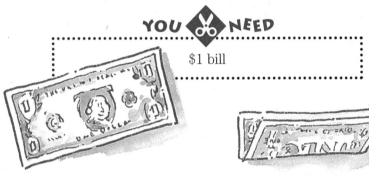

■ Hold a $1 bill right side up, with the picture of George Washington facing you. Fold it in half lengthwise by bringing the bottom to the top (a).

Fold it in half again, bringing the right side back *behind* the left side (b). Fold it in half yet again, this time bringing the right side in front of the left (c).

■ Open the bill by unfolding from the left side to the right (d) and the left side to the right again (e). Then fold the top edge down. George will be upside down (f)!

VANNA VANISHES

All great magicians have an elaborate vanishing act in their bag of tricks. But even up-and-comers can perform this one, and no special equipment is necessary. Here's how to make Vanna vanish.

YOU ✂ NEED

Construction paper or notebook paper •
• Scissors • Felt-tipped markers

■ Make a square from a piece of construction paper (or from a piece of notebook paper) by folding the corner of one short side to the opposite long side and cutting off the excess paper.

■ From the excess paper, cut a small face shape and draw in features to make Vanna.

■ Fold the square in half diagonally and put Vanna inside near the fold (a). Roll up the paper starting at the long edge. As you get to the point, hold the top layer of paper against the tube of paper as you roll the bottom layer under the tube, keeping the paper close to the tabletop (b).

■ Pulling the bottom point toward you and the top point away, open the paper and poof! Vanna has vanished! (The face is still there. It's on the table, under the paper.)

THE JACKS
TELL ALL

Mondo the Magnificent (that's you!) divides a deck of cards into four piles. A friend looks at and remembers the top card in each pile, without showing them to Mondo. Mondo gathers the cards up and picks out the top cards. Magnificent! (Applause.) Here's how it's done.

YOU ❖ NEED

Deck of cards

■ Before you begin, place the four jacks on the top of the deck. Only you know these cards are there.

■ When you perform, start making four piles by placing the top four cards (the jacks) on the table. Build up the piles by placing several cards on each pile until all the cards have been used.

■ Ask your friend to look at the top card in each pile but not to show them to you.

■ Gather up the cards by placing one pile on top of the next. This way, a jack will be on top of the top card in each pile.

■ Spread the deck out in your hands. The four top cards will be the first card on the left (the top card in the first pile) and the three cards to the right of the three jacks.

Pull these cards out of the deck, place them on the table, and bask in the glow of your friend's amazement.

THE PSYCHIC

Mondo the Magnificent is back with another card trick. This time Mondo—you, of course—finds the one card in a deck of 52 that the audience "volunteer" has chosen. Here's how.

YOU ✄ NEED

> Deck of cards

■ Shuffle a deck of cards so that the cards are in no particular order. Then fan them out, facedown, in front of a friend. Ask him to choose a card and remove it from the deck.

■ As he looks at the card, pick up the deck and straighten it. As you do, look at the bottom card (don't make it obvious that you are looking) and remember what it is. Put the deck facedown on the table in one pile and have your friend put the card back, facedown, on top of the deck.

■ Ask your friend to cut the cards by taking the top part of the deck and putting it next to the other part of the deck. You finish the cut by placing the rest of the cards on top of the pile he moved.

■ Now, slowly fan out the deck faceup as you pretend to be psychic. The card that your friend chose is the one that is on top of the card you memorized.

Try this trick several times with the same person. Each time you will be able to identify the chosen card simply by remembering what card was on the bottom of the deck before the deck was cut.

COLUMN BY COLUMN

Here's another card-identifying trick Mondo the Magnificent can pull on an unsuspecting friend.

YOU ✄ NEED

Deck of cards

1. Shuffle a deck of cards, if you know how. If not, just turn them facedown and mix them up with your hands. Put three cards faceup on the table. Overlap three more cards on top of these, and continue until you have three columns of seven cards each. Put the rest of the deck aside.

2. Ask a friend to choose a card but not to remove it from the column or tell you which one it is. Just ask her which column it is in.

3. As you pick up the cards, you want the column with your friend's card in it to be in the middle—not the first column you pick up and not the last. Pick up the cards, sliding the cards in each column together so that they stay in the same order.

4. Turn the pile of cards facedown in your hands, and again make three columns with the cards facing up. Ask your friend which column her card is in. Pick up the cards, again making sure the column with her card in it is in the middle.

5. Make three columns for a third time and ask your friend where her card is. Pick up the cards so that her column is in the middle.

6. Turn the cards facedown. Then turn them over one at a time. As you get to the eleventh card, ask your friend if that is her card. She will be amazed that you picked the right card. The chosen card is always the eleventh card.

KNOT? NOT!

Sometimes things aren't what they seem. For instance, you can tie what appears to be an elaborate set of knots. But a mere pull on the ends of the string and presto—they're gone. Here's how.

YOU ◆ NEED

String

■ With a 1-foot-long piece of string, tie an overhand knot with the right end over the left. Do not tighten it; leave a loop at the bottom. Tie another overhand knot above it, this time left over right. Again, leave a loose loop (a).

■ Now, take the right end of the string. First put it through the bottom loop from front to back (b).

■ Then bring the end up and right, outside the knots, and go through the top loop, again from front to back (c).

■ Now, slowly pull on the ends of the string and straighten it. The knots disappear!

These are right-handed directions. If you're a left-handed magician, reverse them. Substitute "left" for "right" and "right" for "left" to make the trick work.

LOOPY LOOPS

Mondo the Magnificent (you again!) shows friends a loop made of newspaper. Mondo asks how many loops there will be if the loop is cut lengthwise down the middle. The audience says two. Mondo cuts the loop and shows the audience two separate loops.

Mondo starts to cut another loop and asks the same question. Everyone predicts two loops. But, by magic, Mondo shows them one big loop.

Finally, Mondo starts to cut a third loop and again asks how many loops there will be. Some say one, others two. This time, Mondo shows them two loops—that are linked together! Here's how to do it.

YOU  NEED

Newspaper • Transparent tape • Scissors

■ You need to set up the three loops before you perform. Cut them out of newspaper. Each loop should be about 2 inches wide (wide enough to cut lengthwise) and 2 or 3 feet long.

■ To make the first loop, bring the ends together and tape them (a).

a

MÖBIUS STRIP
A unique loop, indeed.

The second loop in the Loopy Loops trick—the one with one twist before you tape the ends—is called a Möbius strip. It is named after its discoverer, August Ferdinand Möbius, a German mathematician who lived from 1790-1868.

This strip is unique because it is a one-sided surface. You can see this for yourself by making a line down the center of the strip with a marker or a pen.

Place the pen at one point on the strip and, without lifting the pen, go around the strip. You will end up at the same point you began. Even though the strip looks as if it has a line down both its "sides," it has only one side.

To make the second, bring the ends together, twisting one end before you tape them (b).

b

For the third loop, twist one end twice before you tape the ends together (c).

c

THE HIDDEN PENNY

You can put a penny in your pocket and then make it look as if it jumped from your pocket back into your hand. To do this, you need to layer in the palm of your hand a penny, a quarter, and another penny. Make sure the bottom penny is hidden by the quarter.

YOU NEED
• Two pennies and a quarter

■ Open your hand and pick up the top penny, holding it up so that everyone can see it. Put the top penny in your pocket. As you do this, close your hand and roll the coins around so that the bottom penny is now on top of the quarters.

■ Ask your friend where the penny is. She'll say it's in your pocket. Open your hand and, by magic, the penny is back in your hand!

BANANA SPLIT

Split a banana with your finger—while it's still inside its skin! Impossible, your audience says? Not for the world's great new magician—you. But you will need to prepare the banana ahead of time.

YOU ✄ NEED

Banana • Sewing needle • Thread

■ To prepare the banana, thread a sewing needle with a single length of thread. Do not knot the end.

■ Take a shallow ½-inch stitch, so that the needle goes under the banana skin, not into the banana. Leave a 3-inch tail of thread. Put the needle back into the hole it just came out of, and make another shallow stitch.

■ Continue making shallow stitches around the banana, each time putting the needle back in the same hole it came out of. When you come back to the first hole, pull the needle through it. You now have a loop of thread surrounding the banana underneath the skin.

■ Pull the two pieces of thread that stick out of the first hole; the thread will cut through the banana. (You can discard the thread.) The holes in the banana skin will not show.

■ To present this trick, say, "I can cut this banana with my finger because I know the magic word." Say your magic word, then place your finger on the banana where you made the stitches. Now, open the banana skin, and show the audience a banana that is indeed split!

KEEP IT DRY

To practice for the day when you pull a rabbit out of a hat, pull a dry tissue out of a cup of water. Every great magician has to start somewhere! Here's how.

YOU  NEED

Two 10-ounce paper cups • Three small 5-ounce paper cups • Masking tape • Measuring cup (optional) • Tissues

To prepare for this trick, you will need to make special cups. Take two large (at least 10-ounce) paper cups, and tape a smaller 5-ounce cup inside the base of each one. (Wrap a piece of tape around the small cup and attach the ends of the tape to the inside of the large cup.) Make sure that the small cups are really secure and that they are as far down inside the large cups as possible. You don't want your audience to see them.

Perform this trick as follows:

■ Put about ¼ cup of water in a measuring cup or in another 5-ounce paper cup.

■ Put a dry tissue into each doubled cup. Only you know that you are carefully tucking the tissues into the small paper cups. Then pour the water slowly into one of the larger cups, being careful not to get any in the small cup holding the tissue. (It's smart to practice pouring a few times before you perform the trick.) Ask the audience, "Is water wet?" Of course, they will say yes.

■ Pour the water slowly from the large cup into the other large cup, again being careful not to get any water in the small cup. Then pull the dry tissue out of the first cup. As the audience looks on in amazement, pull the dry tissue out of the second cup.

THE UNPOPPABLE BALLOON

Blow up several balloons and give them to your friends along with a straight pin. Tell your friends that if they know the right magic words, they can stick a pin in a balloon without popping it. Have several of your friends try. Of course, all the balloons will pop. Now stick a pin in your balloon. It doesn't pop!

YOU NEED
- Balloon
- Transparent tape
- Straight pin

The secret to this trick is to put a small piece of transparent tape on your balloon. When you stick the pin through the tape—and don't pull it out—the balloon won't pop.

RAINY-DAY BANDSTAND

Wouldn't a jam session liven things up on a dull, rainy day? What if you were the leader of the band? Music can get you going, and playing tunes on homemade instruments adds to the fun. Invite friends over to make one or more of the instruments described here from things you have around the house. If you like, you can decorate instruments like the kazoo, guitar, or xylophone with poster paint, markers, or stickers. Just be sure to let everything dry before you strike up the band!

GLASS CHIMES

These chimes sound great and you can use them to water the plants when the concert's over.

The most melodious sounds are made with the thinnest glass, so choose glasses that are thinner than a jar or a jelly glass. But don't use the family's best glassware! (It's best to check with an adult before you use any glasses.)

YOU NEED

Eight glasses • Water • Food coloring (optional) • Teaspoons

■ Line up eight glasses of about the same size and shape. Fill the first ⅛ full of water for the high note, the second ¼ full for the next note, the third ⅜ full for the next note, and so on. The eighth glass should be full.

■ Using the musical scale *do, re, mi, fa, sol, la, ti, do,* make the full glass *do,* the ⅞-full glass *re,* the ¾-full glass *mi,* and so on. The ⅛-full glass is *do* again. "Tune" the glasses by adding or removing water so that each note rings true in the scale. To make your chimes more attractive, add a few drops of a different food coloring to each glass.

■ Use a metal teaspoon on the rims of the glasses to gently tap out a song. Start with simple songs like "Mary Had a Little Lamb" and "Hot Cross Buns," and then work up to an old favorite like "Oh! Susanna."

KOOKY KAZOOS

Turn a collection of empty tubes from paper towels, toilet paper, waxed paper, and aluminum foil into kazoos. Kazoos are tube-shaped instruments that you hum into to make a funny sound that is somewhere between a horn and a human voice.

YOU NEED

Cardboard tubes • Waxed paper • Scissors • Rubber bands • Ruler • Pencil

To make a kazoo, measure and cut a 5-inch square of waxed paper, place it over one end of an empty tube, and attach it with a rubber band.

To play your kazoo, hum a tune gently into the open end of the tube—the waxed paper will vibrate and make your tune sound musical. If you have friends over, take turns choosing favorite songs for the whole group to play and strike up the kazoo band!

A DRUM
TO KEEP THE BEAT

Drums have been used for centuries in many ways—to send messages, as a call to battle, in religious ceremonies, to keep the beat for dancers, and in celebrations and festivals. They're fun and easy to play.

For this drum, a cylindrical oatmeal container forms the body, and layers of brown paper form the drumhead, the part you beat. Layering the paper makes the drumhead stronger, and the combination of the paper layers and the air spaces between them lets you create deeper sounds on the drum than a single layer of paper would.

■ First, find a pie plate or lid from a cooking pot that is about 4 inches larger in diameter than the top of the oatmeal container, to use as a tracing template. Trace five or six circles onto brown paper, then cut them out.

■ Put one paper circle on top of the open end of the oatmeal container and tape the edge to the side of the container, making folds along the edge so that it lies flat. Smooth white glue on the top of the paper and place the second circle on it, again taping the edges to the side of the container. Continue gluing and taping the circles.

■ Allow the glue to dry. You can paint and decorate the oatmeal container, but don't paint the brown paper.

■ To make a strap for hanging, tape the ends of a 1- or 1½-yard-long piece of rope,

YOU ❖ NEED

Cylindrical oatmeal container • Pie plate or pot lid • Pencil • Brown wrapping paper or grocery bags • Scissors • Tape • White glue • Wooden spoon • Cotton balls • Ruler • Fabric scrap • Rubber band • Rope, ribbon, leather thong, or lanyard

decorative ribbon, leather thong, or lanyard to the sides of the oatmeal container.

■ To make a drumstick, measure and cut a 6-inch square of fabric. Place several cotton balls in the center of the fabric and then put the bowl of a wooden spoon on top of them. Place some more cotton balls on the back of the bowl, gather up the fab-

ric, and secure it to the spoon handle with a rubber band.

■ To play the drum, place the strap over your right shoulder (if you are right-handed) and hold the drum at your left side. Use your right hand to hold the drumstick. If you are left-handed, place the strap over your left shoulder, and play with your left hand.

MERRY MARACAS

In some countries, you're never too old to play with rattles. Take Brazil, for example, where no band would be complete without a maraca player. Maracas are percussion instruments usually made of hollowed-out gourds filled with pebbles or dried beans—basically, big rattles. They are always played in pairs—one maraca in each hand—so make sure you make two for each person.

■ A simple way to make maracas is with paper or disposable plastic drinking cups. You will need two cups for each maraca, or four cups for each set. You can decorate the cups with markers if you wish.

■ Put about ¼ cup of uncooked rice in one cup, turn the second cup upside down on top of the first one, and put cloth tape (available at hardware stores) around the cups where the rims meet. Wrap the tape around twice to make sure the seam is secure. Make a second maraca the same way, then shake away.

YOU ✄ NEED

Paper or plastic cups • Uncooked rice (or dried beans, lentils, pasta, popcorn kernels, sand) • Cloth tape • Scissors • Felt-tipped markers (optional)

Try putting dried beans, lentils, dried pasta, popcorn kernels, even sand inside different pairs and listen to the different sound each material makes.

TINKLY TAMBOURINE

A tambourine adds a sweet sound to your band. A tambourine is actually a type of frame drum, a drum where the drumhead—the part you beat—is stretched over a frame. Of course, a tambourine has the extra sound of the objects you attach around the edge.

YOU NEED

Aluminum foil pie plate • Hole punch • String • Buttons • Bells

■ With a hole punch, punch 10 or 12 holes evenly around the edge of an aluminum foil pie plate. Thread a piece of string about twice as long as the outside edge of the plate through one hole. Slip a bell or a button with a large hole onto the string, then thread the string through the next hole in the plate. Alternate bells and buttons around the plate. When you're done, tie the thread ends together.

■ To play your tambourine, shake the plate to rattle the buttons and bells as you tap the plate gently against your wrist or thigh. Shake, rattle, and roll!

RUBBER BAND GUITAR

A homemade guitar can be fun to play even if you don't get the rich, melodic sounds of a real guitar.

YOU NEED

Ruler • Pencil • Shoe box • Craft knife or scissors • Paper towel tube • Masking tape • Four large rubber bands • Two unsharpened pencils • Poster paint, brushes, brown wrapping paper, felt-tipped markers (optional)

■ To begin, measure and draw a 4- to 6-inch circle or rectangle on the top of a shoe box lid. The size will depend on the size of your shoe box. Make sure to leave a border at least 2 inches wide all around the edge of the circle or rectangle.

■ In the center of one end of the shoe box bottom, trace a circle around one end of a paper towel tube. Ask an adult to help you cut out the holes with a craft knife.

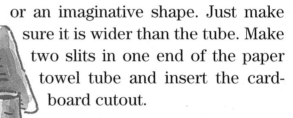

■ To make a decorative head for the neck of the guitar, use the cardboard you cut out of the lid. Cut it into a triangle, circle, or an imaginative shape. Just make sure it is wider than the tube. Make two slits in one end of the paper towel tube and insert the cardboard cutout.

■ Put the lid on the shoe box and push the paper towel tube through the hole in the end of the box. Tape the lid and tube securely in place.

■ Slide the rubber bands over the box lengthwise. If you're using rubber bands of different thicknesses, start with the thickest rubber band and end with the thinnest. Keep the rubber bands about ½ inch apart so that you have strumming room.

■ To get the best sound, insert pencils under the rubber bands at the top and bottom of the hole. If your rubber bands are the same thickness, insert the top pencil at an angle, so that the parts of the rubber bands you strum are different lengths. (Rubber bands of different thicknesses automatically produce different notes.)

■ If you like, paint the guitar with poster paint before you attach the rubber bands, and you can cover the pencils with construction paper in a color that matches the paint. Or cover the box with brown wrapping paper and decorate it with markers.

QUICK TRICK

YOU'VE GOT RHYTHM

Here are two percussive instruments that are quick to make and will fill out the sounds of any band.

YOU NEED
- Paper plates
- Crayons or markers
- Bells
- Stapler
- Pot lids
- Wooden spoon

SHAKER BELLS

Make a simple noise-maker that is part tambourine and part maraca.

■ Decorate the under-side of two paper plates with crayons markers. Then turn over one plate and place three small bells in the center. Put the second paper plate on top of the first, and staple the plates together along the outside edge. Now shake the plates gently and listen to the rhythm of the bells.

CYMBALS

■ For the loudest of musical sounds, use two same-size metal pot lids as cymbals. Don't use enameled lids because they may chip. (Check with an adult before using any lids.)

■ If this sound drowns out the rest of the instruments, try tapping one pot lid lightly with a wooden spoon.

NAILHEAD
XYLOPHONE

Here's your chance to hammer out your favorite tune: Build a xylophone with nails for the bars. Ask an adult to help you hammer in the nails.

YOU NEED

Plywood • Ruler • Pencil • Nails • Hammer • Dowel

■ To make your xylophone, first assemble and size your materials. The plywood should be 2 inches thick (you can use two 1-inch thick pieces) and measure about 5 by 15 inches. You'll need four 3-inch nails and four 2½-inch nails. For the mallet, you'll need a 4-inch nail and a 5-inch length of 1-inch-thick dowel.

■ Draw a line lengthwise down the center of the plywood. Starting about 2 inches in from one end, place a 3-inch nail on the line and carefully hammer its tip into the wood just far enough so that it stands up about 2½ inches. Place the next 3-inch nail about 1½ inches away,

and hammer it down ¼ inch lower than the first nail.

■ Continue the same way with the other two 3-inch nails. Place them 1½ inches apart and hammer each one ¼ inch lower than the one before. Switch to the shorter nails and hammer each one so that it is 1½ inches away from and ¼ inch lower than the one before. When you are finished, you will have hammered eight nails, each 1½ inches apart.

■ To make the mallet, carefully hammer the nail into one end of the dowel, leaving about 3 inches of nail showing. To play the xylophone, tap the nail end of the mallet against the nails in the board.

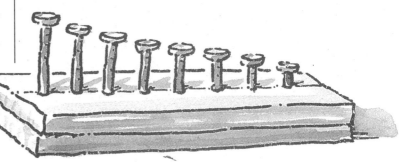

NUMBER FUN

Almost everything can be weighed, measured, or counted in some way. In fact, it's hard to imagine a world without numbers. Besides telling us something we need to know, numbers can be fun! And if the words *fun* and *numbers* don't seem to add up, remember this: You couldn't get your allowance without numbers. Or have a birthday. Or turn to your favorite channel. These tricks and games will give your mind a real workout. You need a calculator for some of them, paper and pencil for others— and your brain for all of them.

NUMBER ONE

Here's an easy math problem where the answer is always 1.

YOU NEED

Paper • Pencil

1. Ask a friend to choose a number from 1 through 10 but not to tell you what it is.

2. Have your friend double the number.

3. Tell your friend to add 2.

4. Ask your friend to divide the answer in step 3 by 2.

5. Tell her to subtract the original number from that result. Tell your friend that the answer is 1.

Here's an example:
1. Your friend chooses 6.
2. 2 x 6 = 12
3. 12 + 2 = 14
4. 14 ÷ 2 = 7
5. 7 – 6 = 1

FOREVER 37

In this math problem, the answer is always 37, no matter what the question.

1. Choose any number from 1 through 9 and multiply it by 3. Say you choose 7.

$7 \times 3 = 21$

2. Make a 3-digit number using the original number three times.

777

3. Now divide the answer in step 2 by the answer in step 1.

$777 \div 21 = 37$

Now try it with 4.

$4 \times 3 = 12$

$444 \div 12 = 37$

It works every time!

QUICK ⏱ TRICK

NUMBER PALINDROME

A number palindrome is a number that reads the same backward as it does forward. In this game, you always end up with a number palindrome.

1. Start with a 3- or 4-digit number, say 153.

2. Reverse it: 351.

3. Add the two numbers: 153 + 351 = 504.

4. Reverse the answer number and add the two numbers: 504 + 405 = 909.

You may have to repeat the last step several times, but you'll always eventually end up with a number palindrome.

TAKE IT
TO THE NINES

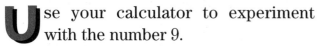

U se your calculator to experiment with the number 9.

1. Choose any number that has all nines in it, for example 99,999.

2. Multiply it by any number, say 17, and write down the answer.

99,999 x 17 = 1,699,983

3. Add the digits in the answer.

1 + 6 + 9 + 9 + 9 + 8 + 3 = 45

4. Add the answer digits again.

4 + 5 = 9

You may have to add the answer digits once or twice more, but you will always end up with 9.

Try this yourself with a different number of nines, say 999,999, and any other number you choose.

A MAGIC NUMBER

The number 123,456,789 is a magic number when multiplied. Try this and see what happens.

1. Choose any number from 1 through 9, say, 4.

2. Multiply the magic number by the number you chose.

123,456,789 x 4 = 493,827,156

3. Multiply the answer in step 2 by 9.

9 x 493,827,156 = 4,444,444,404

You will always get a 10-digit number. Nine digits will be the same as the number you chose in step 1, and there will always be a zero in the tens place.

To work this problem on a calculator, you need one with a 10-digit display. If your calculator has a display of only 8 digits, you'll have to work it out with paper and pencil!

THE SUM OF THEM

Play this number game with a friend. The first time you, do he or she will think you're a numbers wizard!

1. You will need five small pieces of paper or index cards. On the first piece, write 1 on the front and 2 on the back. On the second piece, write 3 on the front and 4 on the back. On the next piece, write 5 and 6, on the next 7 and 8, and on the last 9 and 10.

2. Give the pieces of paper to your friend, and ask her to mix them up. Without looking at what she's doing, have your friend spread the papers out with either side turned up. Ask your friend how many odd numbers are faceup. When you know how many odd numbers are up, you will be able to tell your friend the sum of all the numbers showing.

3. Here's how you do it: The sum of all the even numbers is 30.

$$2 + 4 + 6 + 8 + 10 = 30$$

For each odd number showing, subtract 1 from 30, because each odd number is one less than the even number on the reverse of the paper. So if three odd numbers are showing, subtract 3 from 30 to get 27. The numbers showing could be

$2 + 4 + 5 + 7 + 9$ *or*

$1 + 3 + 5 + 8 + 10$

or any other combination of two even numbers and three odd numbers. In all cases, the total is 27.

If only one odd number is showing, the answer is 29 (30 − 1). If all 5 odd numbers are showing, the answer is 25 (30 − 5).

TOOTHPICK TALLY

Here's a counting trick to play with two friends. Have them sit at a table with a box of toothpicks. You face away from the table. You'll be able to tell how many toothpicks one player has left without knowing how many he started with!

YOU NEED

Toothpicks

1. Ask Player One to choose any number of toothpicks from 10 through 20.

2. Ask Player Two to count the toothpicks Player One chose and then to take twice that number.

3. Have Player One give 3 toothpicks (or any number from 1 through 10 that you choose) to Player Two.

4. Ask Player Two to count how many toothpicks Player One has left, and to give him twice that number from her own toothpicks.

Now, tell Player Two that she has 9 toothpicks left—and she does! The trick is that Player Two will always end up with three times the number Player One gave her in step 3:

$$3 \times 3 = 9$$

Play the game again, having your friends choose a different number to start with.

1. Player One chooses 12 toothpicks.

2. Player Two takes 24.

3. Ask Player One to give 7 to Player Two. (Player One will have 5 left; Player Two will have 31.)

4. Player Two gives 10 toothpicks (2×5, the number Player One has left) to Player One. Player One now has 15 toothpicks and Player Two has 21, or 3 times the number in step 3:

$$3 \times 7 = 21$$

HOW MANY YOU'S?

Set up your own measuring system using your body rather than a ruler or yardstick.

YOU NEED

String or yarn • Paper • Pencil

■ Use a piece of string or yarn to measure around your head. How many lengths will it take to equal your height? Then use your height to measure the basement or play-room. Lie down and see how many times your body will fit across the room, in both directions.

■ What happens if you use the length of your foot as the first measurement? How many of your "feet" tall are you? How many "feet" long is the room?

If your sister or brother is shorter than you, try measuring the length of the hall with them.

FOUR EVERMORE

Here's a trick in which you write a number as numerals and then as words and count the letters. You always end up with 4!

YOU  NEED

Paper • Pencil

■ Let's say you choose 189. Write the number in numerals: 189.

Then, write the word: *one eighty-nine* (*one hundred eighty-nine* will also work).

Now, count the letters: 13 (Don't count the space between *one* and *eighty*, and you don't count the hyphen.)
Write the word: *thirteen*
Count the letters: 8
Write the word: *eight*
Count the letters: 5
Write the word: *five*
Count the letters: 4

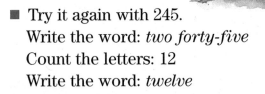

■ Try it again with 245.
Write the word: *two forty-five*
Count the letters: 12
Write the word: *twelve*

Count the letters: 6
Write the word: *six*
Count the letters: 3
Write the word: *three*
Count the letters: 5
Write the word: *five*
Count the letters: 4
It works every time!

QUICK TRICK

GAME OF 20

Here's a fun counting game to play with a partner. The object is to be the person who says 20.

■ You take turns, and at each turn you may count one or two numbers. You say 1, the other player says 2, 3; you say 4, 5, the other player says 6; and so on.

■ The key to winning is to be the player who gets to 17. If you say 17, the other player can say either 18 or 18, 19. You can then say either 19, 20 or 20—and win the game!

INCREASE
YOUR ALLOWANCE

If you offered to do your chores for a penny the first day and doubled your fee on each following day—1¢ to 2¢ to 4¢, and so on—how long would it take you to become a millionaire? You may think you could never earn $1,000,000 by starting with a penny, but work out the figures.

YOU  NEED

Paper • Pencil • Calculator

If you are paid 1¢ the first day, 2¢ the second day, 4¢ the third day, 8¢ the fourth day, 16¢ the fifth day, 32¢ the sixth day, and 64¢ the seventh day, you will earn only $1.27 the first week.

But by continuing to double the amount each day, you will earn $162.56 for the second week and $20,807.68 for the third week. Your total for three weeks is an impressive $20,971.51!

So when will you earn your first million? You'll be a millionaire in less than a month. By the end of the twenty-seventh day, you will have earned more than $1,000,000.

GREAT MEMORY!

Show your friends what a great memory you have!

YOU NEED

Paper • Pencil

1. Ask a friend to write down a number with at least 10 digits. Say he writes 873,093,428,712. Ask him to read the number aloud, very slowly, digit by digit, because you're going to memorize it.

2. Ask him to cross out one digit and read aloud the new number *in any order* so that you can memorize that as well.

3. Say your friend reads 37,830,942,721. Explain that you will compare the two numbers in your mind and tell him the digit that's missing. In just a second you tell him the number 8 was crossed out.

4. Here's how you do it: When your friend reads the first long number very slowly, you don't memorize it. Instead, you use the time to add it up in your head:

$$8 + 7 + 3 + 0 + 9 + 3 + 4 + 2 + 8 + 7 + 1 + 2 = 54$$

Remember *that* number: 54. Then, when your friend reads out the second number, add that up:

$$3 + 7 + 8 + 3 + 0 + 9 + 4 + 2 + 7 + 2 + 1 = 46$$

5. In your head, subtract the smaller number from the larger number: $54 - 46 = 8$. The difference in the two totals is the number your friend crossed out.

It requires a bit of work, but it's easier than memorizing a 12-digit number, then figuring out the 11 numbers that aren't missing!

BIRTHDAY
MATH

In this game, you have a friend do some calculations. From the answer, you can tell your friend her birthdate and her age (even if you don't already know).

YOU ✂ NEED

Paper • Pencil • Calculator (optional)

1. Have your friend write her birthdate in numbers. This means that the month and day are written as numbers: 1 for January, 2 for February, 7 for July, and so on. Right next to that, ask her to write the day of her birth in two digits. If the date is a single digit—1 through 9—she should put a zero in front of it. For 7, she should write 07, for example. This way, 1011 is October 11th and 703 is July 3rd. Ask your friend to keep the answers to steps 1 through 5 secret from you.

2. Ask her to multiply her birthdate number by 2.

1,011 x 2 = 2,022

3. Next, she adds 5.

2,022 + 5 = 2,027

4. Then, she takes the answer in step 3 and multiplies it by 50.

2,027 x 50 = 101,350

5. Finally, she adds her age to that number and then tells you the answer.

101,350 + 8 = 101,358

6. Now it's your turn. Subtract 250 from your friend's answer, and you can tell her birthdate and age.

101,358 – 250 = 101,108

The last two digits are your friend's age (08 means she's 8 years old), and the first four digits, 1011, tell you that her birthdate is October 11th.

KNICKKNACKS

& ARTIFACTS

When you make something yourself, it's fun, it's rewarding, and it gives you a feeling of pride. Make something beautiful, like a mosaic planter or a dip-dyed greeting card. Make something amusing, like papier-mâché masks or ice-cube candles. Make something useful, like refrigerator magnets or a portfolio. Just follow the step-by-step directions, and choose the colors, decide on the texture, create the decoration, add your own special touch.

SILVER LANTERN

Pierce a disposable aluminum foil pan that's at least 6 by 9 inches with tiny holes and add a glowing candle and you'll really light up a room.

1. First, draw a design for the lantern's holes on a piece of 6- by 9-inch paper. Keep the design simple, just the outline of shapes like flowers, leaves, fish, snowflakes—or monster faces.

2. Then with scissors cut a 6- by 9-inch rectangle from the bottom of the pan. Place your design on top of the aluminum rectangle and place both design and foil on top of a thick pile of newspapers.

3. With a hammer and nail, gently punch holes along the lines of your design. (Ask an adult assistant to help you here.) Don't

hammer too hard! You want small holes with some space between them. If the holes are too close together, they will join together into one big hole.

4. When you have finished punching your design, make a hole in each corner of the rectangle. Shape the lantern by wrapping it around a large can, like a can of beans or coffee. Once the foil is rounded, remove it from the can and overlap the short ends so that the holes in the two ends meet. Insert a brass paper fastener through each pair of holes, being sure to go through both layers of foil. To secure, open the prongs on the inside of the foil.

5. To make a candle holder, place a candle 2½ to 3 inches long (shorter than the lantern) in a disposable aluminum cupcake or muffin cup. To keep the candle upright, light the candle and drip some wax into the center of the muffin cup. (Ask your assistant for help with melting the wax.) Blow out the candle, then place it in the melted wax and hold it there for a minute. As the wax hardens, it will hold the candle in place.

Place the lantern over the candle. When you light the candle, your design will shine.

QUICK TRICK

PENNY BOOKMARK

It's simple to make an impressive-looking bookmark with only a large paper clip and two pennies. (You may want to clean the pennies first [page 79] so that they're nice and shiny.) The bookmark slips onto the page to keep your place.

■ To glue the pennies to the paper clip, put a dab of Duco® cement (or any glue that works on metal) on the center of one of the pennies. Place the end of the paper clip with one loop (not two) on top of the penny. Then put another dab of glue on the second penny and place it over the first penny, sandwiching the top of the paper clip between the pennies. Let the glue dry.

YOU NEED
• Large paper clips
• Pennies or other coins
• Duco® cement

■ You can also use colored paper clips and different kinds of coins—even foreign coins, if you have them.

ICE-CUBE
CANDLES

Ice cubes mixed with melted wax create crevices and caves, making this candle look like a jagged rock formation. Ask an adult to help you work with the hot wax.

YOU NEED

Old crayons • Empty coffee can • Empty 1-quart milk or juice carton • Scissors • Paraffin • Saucepan • Pot holders • Small candle • Ice cubes

1. Peel the paper off three or four old crayon pieces that are the same or similar colors. Wash and dry a coffee can and cut a clean empty 1-quart milk or juice carton down to about 6 inches.

2. To melt the wax, put five or six slabs of paraffin and the crayon pieces into the can. Hot wax can catch fire, so set the can in a pot of water—the water should come halfway up the sides of the can. Ask your helper to heat the pot on the stove. As the water boils, the wax in the can melts.

3. When the wax has melted, turn off the stove, and have your adult assistant pick up the can with pot holders. Be very careful when handling hot wax! Pour about ½ inch of wax into the bottom of the carton. Position a small candle (about ½ inch thick and 4 or 5 inches long) in the center of the carton. As the wax hardens, it will hold the candle in place.

4. Put ice cubes around the small candle. Using pot holders to hold the can, pour the rest of the melted wax over the ice cubes. Let the wax reach the top of the candle without covering the wick.

5. Set the carton aside for about an hour while the wax hardens. Then pour out the water from the melted ice and gently tear away the carton to see the surprising-looking candle you have created.

MOSAIC PLANTERS

Potted plants become works of art when they're tucked inside mosaic planters. These planters, decorated with all sizes and colors of dried beans, are easy to make and are nice gifts.

Choose cans that are short and wide—like the ones nuts come in—so that flowerpots will fit inside them. Medium-size cans (12 to 15 ounces) are good for small plants. You can use dried navy, pinto, kidney, pink, white, and black beans and dried split peas and lentils for your mosaic.

YOU ✂ NEED

Empty cans • Medium-weight sandpaper • Paper towels • Paper • Pencil • White glue • Dried beans • Shellac • Small paintbrush •

1. Wash the cans and remove any paper labels. Sand the outside of the cans with medium-weight sandpaper and wipe them clean with a damp paper towel. Sanding the cans roughs up the surface, giving the glue and beans a better grip.

2. Have a complete design in mind for each can before you start (sketch it first on paper, if you like), but work on only one section of a can at a time. Put glue on one area. Outline the shape you want with the largest beans, gluing them on one at a time. Fill the area inside the outline with smaller beans. Cover the surface completely so that the can doesn't show.

3. When the glue has dried, paint over the design with clear shellac to protect the beans and give a shine to the planter. Let the shellac dry overnight.

DIP-DYED
GREETING CARDS

Why buy plain old greeting cards when you can make groovy ones to send to your friends and relatives?

YOU NEED

Newspapers • Food coloring • Water • Shallow bowls • Plain white paper towels • Construction paper • Scissors • Glue stick • Pen or pencil

1. Cover your table or work space with newspaper. Get out as many shallow bowls as you have colors of food coloring and put a few drops of food coloring in each, using one bowl per color. Add 2 tablespoons of water to dilute the dye.

2. Fold a plain white paper towel four or five times, then dip the corners, edges, and folds into different colors. Open up the paper towel and lay it on the newspaper to dry. Dip more paper towels into different combinations of colors to make lots of different designs.

3. While the paper towels are drying, fold pieces of construction paper in half to form cards. You can use full-size pieces of construction paper, or you can cut pieces to a smaller size or different shape.

4. When the paper towels are dry, cut out the most interesting parts of the designs in rectangles, squares, or unusual shapes. Glue one of the shapes to the center front of the construction paper card. Write your message inside.

QUICK TRICK

THIS IS A STICK-UP!

Refrigerator magnets make a great gift for your parents and grandparents, and they are a handy way to hang your artwork or school papers.

YOU NEED
• Pictures
• Scissors
• White glue
• Cardboard
• Duco® cement
• Magnets

■ To make the magnets, find eye-catching pictures—flowers from a seed catalog, a picture of a car from an advertisement, jungle animals from a nature magazine, or a picture of yourself from a snapshot—and cut them out. Your cutouts should be the size you want the magnets to be.

■ With white glue, glue the pictures to medium-weight cardboard, such as shirt cardboard or oak tag. Carefully cut around each picture, rounding off any sharp edges.

■ With Duco® cement (or any glue that works on metal), glue one or two magnets (available at variety or hardware stores) to the back of the cardboard. Allow the glue to dry for at least 2 hours before using your magnet.

YOUR OWN
PORTFOLIO

It's sometimes difficult to find space for storing all your drawings and paintings. With a large, flat carrying case, called a portfolio, you can store your work and carry it around, too.

YOU ✂ NEED

Poster board • Yardstick • Pencil • Ruler • Scissors • 1-inch-wide cloth tape • 2¼ yards of ribbon • Felt-tipped markers

1. Position a 22- by 28-inch piece of poster board or oak tag so that the short sides are at the top and bottom and the longer edges are at the sides. Using a yardstick or tape measure, find the center of each of the long edges, mark them with a dot, and draw a line between them.

To make a ½-inch spine, draw two lines, each ¼ inch from either side of the center. Score the two lines by holding a ruler on a line and running one point of a pair of scissors along it. (Ask an adult assistant for help with this.) Fold the poster board on these lines, with the score lines on the outside.

2. Lay the board flat again, scored side (outside) up, and cover the spine along the two scored lines with two pieces of cloth tape (available at hardware stores) overlapping each other along the center. This reinforces the spine. Fold the ends of the tape over on the other side (inside) of the board. Now, turn the portfolio over and reinforce the inside of the spine with two

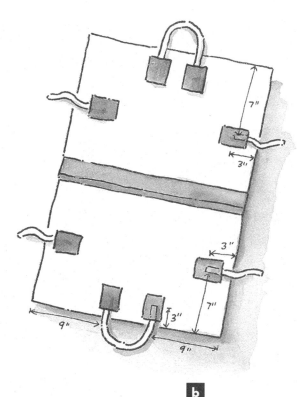

pieces of cloth tape overlapping along the center. Cut them ½ inch short of the edges so they don't fold over to the outside (a).

a

3. Cut the ribbon into four 12-inch pieces for the ties and two 16-inch pieces for the handles. The four shorter pieces will be attached to the sides of the portfolio. Working on the inside, make one mark 7 inches down from the top and one 7 inches up from the bottom on each long side. Place one 12-inch ribbon on each of these marks. About 3 inches of ribbon should be on the poster board. Tape each ribbon to the poster board with cloth tape.

4. For the handle, make a mark 9 inches in from each side on one of the short edges. Place the ends of one 16-inch ribbon on the marks, making a semicircle with 3 inches of each ribbon end on the board, and tape each end. Make another handle on the other short edge (b).

5. With cloth tape, reinforce the outer edges of the portfolio, placing the tape over all the taped ribbons already in place. Turn the portfolio over, and reinforce the outer edges of the outside with cloth tape. Fold the portfolio closed and tie the side ribbons.

Decorate the outside of your portfolio, and write your name or initials on it with markers. You have a handsome personalized portfolio for your work.

b

COLORFUL CLAY
ORNAMENTS

You can create festive ornaments to decorate your room or Christmas tree from easy-to-make cornmeal clay (see the facing page). The tree ornaments make great holiday gifts.

YOU NEED

Cornmeal clay • Newspaper • Waxed paper • Rolling pin or large can • Cookie cutters • Paper clips • Poster paint • Brushes • White glue, glitter, sequins • Clear acrylic paint • Brush • Ornament hooks, string, or leather thong

1. Cover your work area with newspaper. Sandwich each batch of clay between two pieces of waxed paper. Using a rolling pin or a large can, roll the clay out betwen the waxed paper until it is ¼ to ½ inch thick.

2. Remove the top piece of waxed paper and cut out shapes with cookie cutters. If you are making ornaments for your room, use cookie cutters of action fig-

ures and toys. For Christmas ornaments, use cookie cutters in holiday shapes. Push a partially opened paper clip gently into the top of each shape for a hanging loop.

3. Let the clay shapes dry for 1 to 2 hours, or until they are dry to the touch. Decorate them with poster paint or glue glitter, sequins, or other decorations onto them. Let the ornaments dry completely (it might take about 2 days), then protect them with a coat of clear acrylic paint.

To hang an ornament on the Christmas tree, slip an ornament hook through the paper clip hanging loop. To hang an ornament in your room, thread a piece of string or a narrow leather thong through the top of the paper clip hanging loop.

CORNMEAL CLAY

Make multicolored clay that's fun to roll and cut.

INGREDIENTS	KITCHEN TOOLS
¾ cup flour	Waxed paper
½ cup cornmeal	Small plastic
½ cup salt	sandwich bags
Hot water	Large bowl
Food coloring	Measuring cups
	Wooden spoon

1. In a large bowl, mix together the flour, cornmeal, and salt.

2. With a wooden spoon, stir in ¼ cup of hot tap water. Continue adding water a little at a time until the mixture looks like stiff cookie dough. Do not add too much water—dry clay works better than wet.

3. Divide the clay into two or three batches and put each batch on a piece of waxed paper.

4. Make a hole in the center of each batch and add a few drops of food coloring. Roll the clay and knead it to spread the food coloring evenly. Wear small plastic sandwich bags on your hands while you knead the clay to keep the food coloring from staining your hands.

PAPIER-MÂCHÉ
MASK

Some masks disguise, like the one you wear on Halloween. Some masks protect, like the one a baseball catcher wears. And some masks are purely decorative, like this papier-mâché mask that's used as a wall decoration.

1. Cover your work area with newspaper. To make a base for your mask, take a sheet

YOU NEED

Newspaper • Masking tape • Pie plate • Measuring cup • Flour • Water • Spoon • Measuring spoons • White glue • Paper towels • Scissors • Poster paint • Brushes • Clear shellac • Picture hook or nail

of newspaper and scrunch it into a tight egg-shaped base. Put masking tape around the base to hold its shape. Wrap additional sheets of newspaper around the base, securing them with masking tape, until the base is the size you want your mask to be.

2. Tear several sheets of newspaper into 1-inch strips.

3. In a pie plate or other shallow dish, make wheat paste by stirring ¼ cup water into 1 cup of flour. Stir in more water, 1 tablespoon at a time, until the mixture looks like heavy cream. Add a generous squirt of white glue and mix very well.

4. Dip a strip of newspaper into the paste and wipe off the excess by pulling the strip between your fingers. Apply the strip to the front of your newspaper base. Continue adding strips, overlapping them slightly, until the front of the base is covered with two layers of strips—they should extend about as far as the ears go on a head.

5. To create features like eyes, a nose, a mouth, and ears, roll and shape strips of dry newspaper, put the feature in place, and cover and secure it with strips of paste-covered newspaper. Exaggerated features—a bulbous nose, protruding ears, a hat brim, a tongue that sticks out—

add interest to your mask. Just remember to secure the features with several layers of newspaper strips.

When all the features are in place, add two more layers of paste-covered newspaper strips to the whole mask, molding them around the features.

6. For the final layer, place a dry paper towel over the mask. With lots of paste on your fingers, mold the paper towel to the mask, smoothing out wrinkles as you mold. Set your mask aside until it is dry to the touch. This may take several days.

7. When your mask is dry, turn it over and remove the newspaper base. If some of the newspaper sticks to the mask, just tear it off. With scissors, trim the edges of the mask so that they are neat and even.

Paint the mask with poster paint, emphasizing the exaggerated features, if you like. When the paint is dry, add a coat of clear shellac to protect it.

When the shellac is dry, hang the mask on a nail or hook on your bedroom wall where you can admire your creation.

MARBLEIZED
STATIONERY

Transform ordinary white paper and envelopes into elegant stationery with a marbleized trim. This fabulous stationary makes writing even thank-you notes fun!

YOU  NEED

Newspapers • Bucket • Water • Spray paint • White typing or computer paper • Envelopes • Newspaper • Stick, dowel, or chopstick

1. Cover your work area thickly with newspaper. Then, fill an old bucket ¾ full of water. Spray one or more colors of spray paint onto the surface of the water in the bucket. Ask an adult assistant for help with the spray paint. Spray lightly, but cover the entire surface, not just one area.

2. Take a piece of typing or computer paper, and with a smooth, firm motion, dip one corner into the water and out again. The paper will pick up the paint. Repeat with the other corners. Decorate the corners of an envelope to match. Place the paper and envelope on newspaper to dry.

3. When the paint in the bucket coagulates, or dries, it has to be removed. With the stick, lift up the sticky layer of paint and put it on a pile of newspapers.

4. Spray fresh paint on the water, using a different combination of colors, if you like. Try dipping other parts of the paper—the top and bottom edges or one side—into the water. Dip an envelope to match.

IT'S NOT ALL JUNK

Reduce, reuse, recycle! We've all heard the slogan, and we know how important recycling is. It can be fun, too, to find new uses for items we are finished with or would usually throw out. Keep a box full of leftover recyclables, like paper towel tubes, gift wrap, paper, fabric scraps, buttons, small boxes, odd shoe laces, and old game pieces. Then, when you feel creative and want to make something, you will have a box full of materials. Recycled items rescued from the trash can be an inspiration!

LOG CABIN

You can make a log cabin playhouse for your action figure or doll from an old television-set or microwave-oven carton. If you're lucky enough to have a large carton that a refrigerator, dishwasher, or stove came in, you can make a log cabin large enough to play inside yourself.

YOU ✂ NEED

Large carton • Pencil • Ruler • Craft knife • Empty paper-towel, toilet-paper, and wrapping-paper tubes • White glue • Poster paint • Brushes

Plan this project ahead in order to collect enough tubes to cover the carton. Ask friends and neighbors to contribute tubes. Even if you don't have enough to cover your carton, you can get started, and add empty tubes as you collect them.

1. To begin, turn the carton upside down. Measure and mark the opening for the door and windows with a pencil and ruler. Ask an adult assistant to help you cut out the openings with a craft knife.

2. To make the logs, start at the bottom edges of the carton and glue on the tubes. Keep them close together. When the glue is dry, use poster paint to paint the entire cabin light brown and let it dry. If you've made a small house and you have doll-house furniture, put it inside. Or you can make miniature furniture (see page 139). If you've made a big house, put some large pillows inside and enjoy!

DÉCOUPAGE TRAY

écoupage, from the French word that means *to cut*, is an old technique of covering a surface with paper cutouts. A plastic tray—the kind that frozen food comes in—can be made attractive with decoupage and used to hold a collection of coins, jewelry, or paper clips. A découpage tray also makes a great birthday present or end-of-the-year gift for a favorite teacher.

YOU  NEED

Plastic microwave tray • Gift-wrapping paper and old magazines • Scissors • White glue

1. First, neatly cut out motifs and shapes from gift-wrapping paper or magazines. Use soft paper, like gift wrap or magazine pages, rather than stiff paper, like construction paper, so you can mold the paper cutouts around the rounded corners and curved bottom edge of the tray.

2. When you have lots of cutouts—you'll need more than you think!—begin gluing them to the outside sides of the tray, starting just under the lip. Overlap the cutouts so that none of the surface of the tray shows through. Extend the cutouts down the sides and under the bottom edge. Even though the bottom won't show when the tray is placed on a desk or dresser, you can cover the entire bottom with cutouts, if you like. Now cover the inside of the tray with cutouts, starting just under the lip.

When you have covered the entire surface with cutouts—you don't have to do this in one sitting—turn the tray upside down to let the glue dry.

STREETSCAPE

Create a city street, a country village, or a suburban neighborhood with left-over cardboard boxes—shoe boxes, cylindrical oatmeal boxes, Jello and pudding boxes, quart cartons, small jewelry boxes, and paper towel tubes. Some containers, like spaghetti boxes, have ready-made windows covered with cellophane.

YOU  NEED

Brown wrapping paper • Empty cardboard boxes • Pencil • Poster paint • Brushes • Glue • Scissors • Cardboard • Magazines (optional) • Toy cars, toy people (optional)

1. Use a large piece of brown wrapping paper as your base. Decide where you want the streets to be. Pencil them in, and then arrange and adjust the boxes—for buildings, towers, barns, offices, houses, and schools—until you're happy with the layout. Make sure none of the boxes are too large for your streetscape.

2. Put the buildings aside while you paint the paper base. Blend poster paint to make a bluish-gray "asphalt" color. Paint the "streets" on the brown paper and paint white or yellow stripes down the center. For a city street, you won't need to paint much else. For a country village, you'll want more green fields than asphalt streets. To make a suburban setting, border your streets with white sidewalks and green lawns.

3. Paint the boxes to look like buildings— with doors, windows, even curtains, and cats or plants on the windowsills. When the paint is dry, glue the box buildings to the brown-paper base.

4. Now, make details like trees, stop signs, and street-name signs out of cardboard and glue them to your street scene. You can also cut out and glue pictures from magazines to make your streetscape come to life. Add your own toy cars and toy people to complete the scene.

QUICK TRICK

UNLOST GLOVE PUPPET

Make a puppet from two knitted gloves that have lost their mates. (Of course, you can always use a pair of gloves, if you like.)

■ Turn the first glove inside out, leaving the fingers inside. Place this glove on the table with the cuff on top. Put the second glove on the table with the fingers pointing away from you (a).

YOU NEED

• 2 knitted gloves

• Buttons, yarn or fabric scraps (optional)

• White glue (optional)

■ Place the first glove on top of the second one. Bring the middle and ring fingers of the second glove around the first glove. Tie the fingers in an overhand knot (b).

■ Fold the bottom of the first glove up over the knot and pull the cuff down over it, tucking the bottom inside the cuff (c). The cuff becomes the puppet's hat, and the rest of the first glove forms the puppet's head. If you like, you can glue on little buttons, yarn, or fabric scraps to make a face.

To make a pocket for your puppet, tuck in the thumb of the second glove. Slip the puppet on your hand by putting your fingers inside the puppet's "arms."

a

b

c

STAINED-GLASS
WINDOW

If you have ever seen a stained-glass window in a church or museum, you know how magical the light can seem as it streams through the colored glass.

YOU ✂ NEED

Black construction paper • Pencil • Scissors • Ruler • Colored tissue paper • Waxed paper • Iron • White glue • Tape

1. First make the frame. Fold a piece of black construction paper in half, then in half again, then in half a third time—this folds the paper into eighths.

Hold the folded paper so that the last fold you made is on the right side. Measure and mark ½ inch in from the three other sides. Cut out a rectangle (a). Open up the paper. You'll have a frame with four small windows for your stained glass.

2. To make the stained glass, cut leftover scraps of different colored tissue paper into small shapes. Cut two 12-inch lengths of waxed paper. Arrange the tissue paper shapes on one piece of waxed paper. Put the second piece of waxed paper on top.

3. Ask an adult assistant to help you iron over the waxed paper with an iron set at a very low temperature. The heat will melt the wax in the paper, which, when it cools, will keep the tissue in place.

4. Place the black frame on top of the stained-glass paper. Trim the edges of the waxed paper if necessary and glue the frame into place. Tape the stained-glass window to a real window and see what wonderful things it does to the light.

RECYCLED
CRAYONS

If you have bits and pieces of old crayons that are too small to work with, you can make brand-new round ones. Ask an adult assistant for help with the oven steps.

YOU ✄ NEED

Old crayon pieces • Miniature muffin pan • Aluminum foil • Pot holders or oven mitts

1. Peel the paper off all the crayons. Divide the crayon pieces into color families. For example, put pieces of red, pink, maroon, and burgundy crayons in the red group. Sort all the crayon pieces you have in this way.

2. Preheat the oven to 200°F. Line the cups of a miniature muffin pan with pieces of aluminum foil. Let some of the foil extend beyond the top of each muffin cup. Put the crayon pieces from one color family, or from one color if you have enough pieces of one color, in each cup. Put the muffin pan into the oven for 10 minutes.

Use pot holders or oven mitts to remove the muffin pan from the oven and set the pan aside to cool for 30 minutes.

3. When the crayons and the pan are cool to the touch, pull the aluminum foil out of each muffin cup and peel it away from the circular crayon. Voilà! Your old crayon stubs have a new life.

For a really fun new crayon, try using two or three colors in one muffin cup—like blue and green, or yellow, orange, and red. Don't combine more than three colors, or you'll end up with an unattractive, muddy color.

FUNCTIONAL ARTWORK

The pictures that you draw or paint are great for decorating your school notebook, making place mats, or wrapping a present for a special friend.

YOU ✄ NEED

Drawings or paintings • Scissors • Pencil•
Ruler

FOR NOTEBOOK: Clear plastic sheet, Cloth
tape

FOR PLACE MATS: Clear contact paper,
Scissors

FOR GREETING CARDS: White glue,
Construction paper

An Original Notebook

■ Make your notebook a mini-gallery for your latest artworks. To do so, make a reusable window. Measure, mark, and cut a sheet of clear plastic (available at art supply stores) to the same size as the cover of your binder. Use cloth tape to attach the plastic along the top, bottom, and outside edges of the cover. Slip your artwork into the pocket through the open edge near the spine. You can change the look of your notebook every week.

One of a Kind Place Mats

■ For each place mat, you will need a painting or drawing that measures about 12 by 18 inches. Cover the front and back of your artwork with clear contact paper. Trim the edges evenly and round off the corners slightly. You can make as many place mats as you have drawings! You can even make sets of place mats for family meals, birthdays, or other celebrations.

Unique Cards

■ To make a greeting card for a friend's artwork-wrapped birthday present, cut out the most interesting part of a painting and glue it to the front of a piece of folded construction paper. Write your message on the inside. You can slip the card into an artwork envelope (see Fancy Envelopes at right), if you like.

FANCY ENVELOPES

Transform a drawing into an unusual envelope.

1. Make a square piece of paper, one by folding the top left corner of a rectangular piece of paper over to meet the right side and cutting off the excess paper (a).

2. With one corner of the square pointing away from you, place the card in the center of the square and fold the side corners over, leaving enough space for the card to slip in and out (b). Remove the card and open up the paper.

3. Notch the corners, making ½-inch cuts along the fold lines on the top and bottom of both sides. Then make ½-inch cuts in from the sides to meet the first

cuts (c). Remove the small triangles. Fold in the side flaps (d).

4. Fold the bottom flap up, making the fold at the bottom of the side flaps. Cut off the top triangle of the bottom flap, the part that extends above the side flaps (e). Put a thin line of glue along the inside of the side edges of the bottom flap. Fold the flap up and let the glue dry. Then slip your card into the envelope and fold down the top flap. You can tuck the top flap in, or close it with white glue or a fancy sticker.

YOU NEED
- **A piece of paper that is about 1½ times as long as the longer side of your card**
- **Pencil**
- **Scissors**
- **White glue**

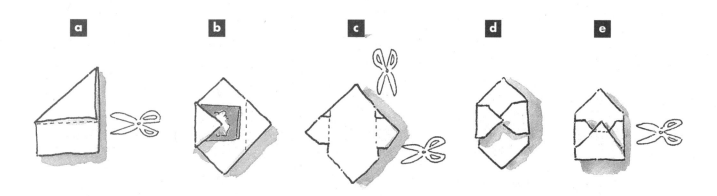

a   b   c   d   e

SCAVENGER MASK

Every face has eyes, nose, mouth, and hair. If you pick up these features from different faces, you can make an extraordinary-looking mask.

YOU NEED

Pencil • Ruler • Newspaper • Scissors • Cardboard • Poster paint • Brushes • Old glossy magazines • White glue • Pencil • Hole punch • Shoelaces or string

1. To make an oval pattern for your mask, measure and cut a 9- by 12-inch piece of newspaper or scrap paper. Fold the paper in half and then in half again, and round off the outside corners with scissors. Open the paper and trace around this oval onto a piece of lightweight cardboard. Then, cut out the shape.

2. Paint the oval any way you like—brown, beige, or pink to look like skin color or an intense green or orange for an alien face. Let the paint dry.

3. While the paint dries, cut out the features you want to use from magazines. (Fashion and celebrity magazines often have full-page faces.) Arrange the features on the painted oval and glue them in place.

If you want to hang the mask, glue a loop of string to the top back of the oval. If you want to wear the mask, bend the cardboard slightly to curve around your face. To make eyeholes, hold the mask up to your face and ask a friend to mark the places for holes with a pencil. Remove the mask and cut out the eyeholes. Punch two holes in the sides of the mask with a hole punch. Tie a shoelace or string through each hole.

JUNK SCULPTURE

Think of all the things that you would ordinarily throw out as raw material for a sculpture.

Start a collection of items like small gift boxes, cardboard tubes, microwave trays, cereal boxes, waxed paper boxes, gift wrap, contact paper, fabric, ribbon, odd game pieces, buttons, shoe laces, sponges, aluminum foil, paper clips, old magazines (and catalogs and newspapers), cotton balls, styrofoam trays, straws, wallpaper scraps, egg cartons, and bottle caps. There's no limit—anything goes.

YOU NEED

Assorted "junk" • White glue • Poster paint • Brushes (optional)

Begin with a flat piece of cardboard as your base and arrange the items you choose into a sculpture, gluing them in place. Or start with a box as your base and glue items to it.

When the glue has dried, you can paint the sculpture with poster paint or leave it in its natural state.

RAINY DAY MENUS

What do you do with a rainy day? There are lots of ways to use this book. You could just thumb through the pages and choose a project that appeals to you. Or you and a friend could turn to the chapter that intrigues you and decide together which project interests you the most. But at other times, it's fun to get together with family and friends to spend an entire afternoon working on an activity. Here are some ideas for just those times. Each menu suggests ways to combine projects in this book that you may not have thought of, and each one will provide you with a fun-filled afternoon, or whole day, or maybe even an entire weekend!

SUPER SPORTS SATURDAY
In the morning (or a day or two before the event):
■ Call your friends to invite them over for an afternoon of sports.

■ Create a sports arena in your playroom or basement. Set up a miniature golf course (page 60), skee ball (page 66), cup catch (page 64), and waste basketball (page 64). You can also turn a hallway into a bowling alley (page 62).

■ Make trail mix (page 117) and frozen bananas (page 116). Collect the ingredients for home-made soda (page 109).

■ Make awards (page 7) for the best rim shot and for a hole-in-one as well as for the player who lost the most balls and the player wearing the most athletic clothing. Have as many awards as there are guests.

As the guests arrive:
Let everyone choose the sport they want to play, and then rotate. If someone seems reluctant to move on to other areas, put a time limit of 15 to 20 minutes on each sport. When everyone has had a chance to play all the games, present the awards. Then make the homemade soda and serve it with the trail mix and frozen bananas.

BABY-SITTER'S GUIDE

If you're stuck inside with some preschoolers on a rainy afternoon, here's a list of games and projects to help you keep them busy.

- Brushless Painting (page 47)
- Mystery Bags (page 36)
- Obstacle Course (page 65)
- Capture Your Shadow (page 76)
- Two-Sided Puzzle (page 32)
- Kooky Kazoos (page 169)
- Junk Sculpture (page 213)

For a snack, make chocolate crunch bars (page 122)—the kids can mix together the different kinds of cereal—and banana smoothies (page 121).

TALENT SHOW

In the morning (or several days) before the event:

- Invite friends over for a planning session.
- Have several people work on a puppet show (page 16).

- Have one or two people practice magic tricks (page 153-166) to perform in the show.
- Write your own lyrics to two or three popular songs (page 15). Practice those songs, as well as some other well-known favorites, so that you can sing for the guests.
- Write a skit using a large cardboard box boat or train (page 12) as the main prop.
- Deliver or send out invitations to the show (page 17).

Just before the event:

- Set up rows of chairs in your playroom, and leave a "stage" area in the front.
- Entertain your friends and neighbors!

MYSTERY AT 245 ELM STREET

Just substitute your own address above, and create an afternoon of mystery at your house!

Several days before the event:

- Write invitations in code (page 35), inviting your friends to an afternoon of mystery. On the bottom of the invitation or on the back, give a clue—A = Z, for example—so your friends can decipher the message.

The morning of the event:

- Set up the games:

- Mystery Bags (page 36)
- Pass It Along (page 38)
- Magazine Scavenger Hunt (page 39)
- Buried Treasure (page 40)
- Capture Your Shadow (page 76)

■ For the treasure hunt (Buried Treasure), make Chocolate Crunch Bars (page 122), wrap each bar in plastic wrap, and place the bars in a treasure box. When it's time to play the game, explain to your guests that the treasure they are hunting for is the snack for the afternoon.

■ Create a mysterious atmosphere in your play-room. Close the window blinds and curtains, turn the lights as low as possible, and play melo-dramatic music—like a Rachmaninoff piano concerto or an E. Power Biggs organ concert—as your guests arrive.

AFTERNOON TEA

In the morning:

■ Invite friends over for make-it-yourself after-noon tea.

In the afternoon:

■ When the guests arrive, have them make their own place mats (page 210). They can take the place mats with them when they go home.

■ Make chocolate chip muffins (page 118).

■ While the muffins are baking, make open-face finger sandwiches. Trim the crusts from white or whole wheat bread and cut the slices into rectangles about 1 inch wide and as long as the slice of bread. Spread each piece of bread with a favorite topping—peanut butter, cream cheese and chives, and sliced cucumbers are all good.

■ Set the table with the handmade place mats.

■ Ask an adult to help you make herb tea. Try chamomile, mint, or raspberry.

■ Serve the finger sandwiches, warm muffins, and tea, and enjoy the afternoon!

GREAT HAIR DAY

Create a beauty parlor in your home and invite several friends over to spend the afternoon get-ting a new hairdo and a manicure.

Before the event:

■ Buy a package of combs (so each guest can have her own comb), ribbons and barrette back-ings to make bow barrettes (page 150), and nail polish and emery boards.

In the morning:

- Invite friends over for a day of beauty.

In the afternoon:

- Have everyone make a bow barrette.

- Divide into pairs and work on each other's hair, creating pony-tails, braids, buns, and other styles using your new bow bar-rettes. Then polish each other's nails.

- If you have an instant camera, take a picture of each guest and give it to her as a memento of the day!

A THOUGHTFUL GESTURE

It's easy to bring a little cheer to the residents of your local nursing home. Take them something to read and a flower to brighten their rooms.

Before the day:

- Collect magazines that your friends and neighbors have finished reading. Get an assortment of news, sports, home, beauty, celebrity, and fashion magazines.

- Collect empty 8-ounce plastic water bottles and leftover yarn.

- Buy colored tissue paper and pipe cleaners.

- Call your local nursing home to arrange a visit.

- Invite friends to your house to make yarn-covered bud vases (page 52) out of the plastic water bottles and yarn.

- Make a tissue paper flower (page 53) for each vase.

On the day:

- Visit the nursing home to take the magazines and give the residents the bud vases and flowers.

YOUR SCHOOL FAIR

Help earn money for your school by making items to sell at the annual fair. Invite some of your friends over to show their school spirit and to make:

- Macramé Key Chains (page 45)
- Mosaic Planters (page 193)
- Safety Pin Bracelets (page 151)
- Money Pouches (page 144)
- Refrigerator Magnets (page 194)

Before the day:

- Collect the empty cans for the planters and the magazines and catalogs for the refrigerator magnets.

- Buy the twine and key rings, dried beans,

safety pins and beads, felt and lanyard, magnets, and lots of white glue.

On the day:
- Cover the table with newspaper.
- Set up five different work areas, one for each project, with all the materials needed for that project. Let guests choose what they would like to work on.
- When everything is dry, put it in a carton or bag to deliver to the school. Your school will be very proud of you!

GRANDPARENTS' DAY

Show your grandparents how much you care by creating a day just for them.

Before the day:
- Call your grandparents on the phone—or visit them if they live close to you—and interview them (page 90).
- Ask an adult to help you write up your notes and make a book of your grandparents' memories (page 130).
- Make a fabric-covered picture frame

(page 96) for a picture of you and your siblings.
- Make a dip-dyed greeting card (page 195).

On the day:
Invite your grandparents to have lunch with you—maybe a lunch you've made yourself. Present them with the book of memories, the picture frame, and the homemade card. How pleased they'll be!

HOLIDAY "SHOPPING"

Start your holiday "shopping" early by making gifts at home. Here are a few suggestions to get you started:

- Marbleized Stationery (page 202)
- Twined Yarn Basket (page 50)
- Straight Curves (page 48)
- A Family Photo Album (page 100)

Now, make a list of your friends and relatives, and decide what you would like to make for each one. List the gifts beside the people. Start making the gifts early enough, and you'll be done before the holiday decorations are in the stores—and that *is* early!

MAIL DELIVERY

If you have a pen pal, regularly write to a favorite cousin, or correspond with a friend who's moved away, make something you can include in a letter (or in a slightly larger envelope) to make your correspondence a little more fun. You could make a two-sided jigsaw puzzle and send the pieces (page 32), create your own cartoon strip (page 128), write a poem (page 132), or send a number puzzle, like a Magic Number (page 181) or Increase Your Allowance (page 186). And, of course, include a picture you have drawn or painted. What a surprise when your correspondent opens the letter!

INDEX

A

Admission tickets, 17
Adventures, 1-22
    Build a Haunted Hallway, 20-22
    Camp In, 4-5
    Create an Artists' Studio, 18-19
    Have an Indoor Parade, 6-7
    Open a Restaurant, 2-3
    Plan a Carnival, 8-9
    Produce a TV Show, 10-11
    Put on a Puppet Show, 16-17
    Take a Cruise…or Ride the Rails, 12-13
    Wake Up to an Opposite Morning, 14-15
Albums:
    for family photos, 100-102
    for special family events, 92-93
Allowance, doubling of, 186
Alphabet, secret code for, 35
Apples, Baked, 113
Apple seeds, sprouting, 75
Artwork:
    body tracings, 77
    brushless painting, 47
    creating studio for, 18-19
    decorating objects with, 210-11
    making portfolio for, 196-97
    setting up gallery for, 18, 19
    silhouettes, 76-77
    string, 48-49
    see also Craft projects;
        Wearable works of art
Awards, 7

B

Backwards, doing things, 14-15
Bags:
    guessing contents of, 36
    lunch, personalized, 143
Baked Apples, 113
Bake sales, 9
Balancing balls race, 68
Balloons:
    making ghosts with, 22
    playing volleyball with, 63
    racing with, 68
    string, 44
    unpoppable, 166
Balloon Volleyball, 63
Banana(s):
    Frozen, 116-17
    Smoothie, 121
    S'Mores, 124
Banana Split (magic trick), 164
Barrettes, bows tied on, 150
Bars, Chocolate Crunch, 122-23
Basketball, indoor version of, 64
Baskets, twined yarn, 50-51
Bath Cents, 79
Beads:
    dough, 146
    magazine, 147
Beanbag toss, clown face, 9
Be an Interior Designer, 139-40
Be a Pen Pal, 136-37
Bells, shaker, 175
Belts, woven with yarn, 54-55
Beverages:
    Banana Smoothie, 121
    Homemade Soda, 109
Bird feeders, 78-79
Bird Food, 79
Birthday Math, 188
Blow Your Stack, 70
Board games:
    Connect Four, 26
    making your own, 24-25
Body tracings, 77
Bookmarks, 191
Botticelli Junior, 27-28
Bottles, plastic:
    bowling indoors with, 62
    volcano in, 70
Bow Barrette, 150
Bowling, 62
Bow Tie Wall Hanging, 94-95
Bracelets:
    friendship, 42-43
    safety pin, 151-52

Brainstorm, 133
Brushless Painting, 47
Bud vases, yarn-covered, 53
Build a Haunted Hallway, 20-22
Buried Treasure, 40

C

Camp In, 4-5
Candles, ice-cube, 192
Capture Your Shadow, 76-77
Cards, greeting. *See* Greeting
    cards
Card tricks:
    Column by Column, 160
    The Jacks Tell All, 158
    The Psychic, 159
Carnival, fund-raising, 8-9
Carrots, growing, 74
Cartons, projects made with:
    log cabin playhouse, 204
    periscope, 72
    puppet stage, 16
    ship or railroad car, 12-13
Cartoon strips, 128
Catch, indoor version of, 64
Chained!, 155
Cheerios challenge race, 68
Cheese:
    Sandwiches, Zesty Toasted,
        111
    Yogurt, 110
Chimes, glass, 168
Chocolate Chip Muffins, 118-19
Chocolate Crunch Bars, 122-23
Christmas tree ornaments, 198-99

Cinquain, 132
Clay:
    cornmeal, 199
    ornaments, 198-99
Clown Face Beanbag Toss, 9
Codes, secret, 35
Collage, 18-19
Color, Moody Blue game and, 28
Colorful Clay Ornaments, 198-99
Column by Column, 160
Connect Four, 26
Cookies, Lemon Drop, 120
Cornmeal Clay, 199
Craft projects, 189-202
    Colorful Clay Ornaments, 198-
        99
    Dip-Dyed Greeting Cards, 194
    Ice-Cube Candles, 192
    Marbleized Stationery, 202
    Mosaic Planters, 193
    Papier-Mâché Mask, 200-201
    Penny Bookmark, 191
    refrigerator magnets, 195
    Silver Lantern, 190-91
    Your Own Portfolio, 196-97
    see also Recyclables, projects
        with; Wearable works of art
Crayons, recycled, 209
Create an Artists' Studio, 18-19
Create a Story, 129
Creative projects, 127-40
    Be an Interior Designer, 139-40
    Be a Pen Pal, 136-37
    Brainstorm, 133
    Create a Story, 129
    Haiku and Cinquain, 132

Keep a Journal, 134-35
Take a Trip To Mars…Back in
    History…, 138
Write and Illustrate a Book,
    130-31
Your Own Cartoon Strips, 128
Cup Catch, 64
Curves, making with straight
    lines, 48-49
Cymbals, 175

D

A Day at the Races, 67-68
A Day in the Life of Your Family,
    88
Découpage Tray, 205
Desserts and snacks:
    Baked Apples, 113
    Banana S'Mores, 124
    Chocolate Chip Muffins, 118-19
    Chocolate Crunch Bars, 122-23
    Frozen Bananas, 116-17
    Fruit Kebabs, 114
    Ice Cream Sandwiches, 125
    Lemon Drop Cookies, 120
    Orange Cream Pops, 115
Dictionary game, 29
Dip-Dyed Greeting Cards, 194
Dollar Bridge, 77
Dough Monster Chain, 146
Drawings:
    decorating objects with, 210-11
    for family or neighborhood
        newspaper, 87
    making portfolio for, 196-97

studio for, 18-19
Dressing up:
  for indoor parade, 6-7
  for TV show, 10-11
Dress-up race, 68
A Drum to Keep the Beat, 170-71

Edible Sprouts, 75
Electromagnet, 73
Envelopes, transforming drawings into, 211

Fabric-covered frames, 96-97
Family history projects, 85-102
  Bow Tie Wall Hanging, 94-95
  A Day in the Life of Your Family, 88
  Family Photo Album, 100-102
  Frame Your Family!, 96-97
  Grow a Family Tree, 98-99
  Interview Your Grandparents, 90-91
  Read All About It!, 86-87
  Relatively Trivial, 89
  Special Event Album, 92-93
Family Photo Album, 100-102
Family trees, 98-99
Fan-folded napkins, 3
Faucets, leaking, 82
Feed the Birds, 78-79
Forever 37, 179
Four Evermore, 185

Frame Your Family, 96-97
Frames:
  decorated oak-tag, 95
  fabric-covered, 96-97
Freaky Folds, 38
French Bread Pizza, 105
Friendship Bracelet, 42-43
Frog race, 68
Frozen Bananas, 116-17
Fruit Kebabs, 114
Functional Artwork, 210-11
Fund-raising, carnival for, 8-9
Furniture, for interior design project, 139-40

Gallery exhibits, 18, 19
Game of 20, 185
Games, 23-32
  Botticelli Junior, 27-28
  Brainstorm, 133
  Connect Four, 26
  Hide in Plain Sight, 37
  Magazine Scavenger Hunt, 39
  Make Your Own Board Game, 24-25
  Moody Blue, 28
  Mystery Bags, 36
  Nim Skills, 31
  Pass It Along, 38
  Relatively Trivial, 89
  Sardines, 66
  Two-Sided Puzzle, 32
  You Don't Know What You're Talking About, 29

  see also Numbers, tricks and games with; Sports, indoor
George Flips!, 156
Ghosts, for haunted hallway, 21, 22
Glass Chimes, 168
Gloves, making puppets with, 207
God's-eyes, miniature, 56-57
Golf, miniature, 60-61
Good Vibes, 84
Grandparents, interview with, 90-91
Great Memory!, 187
Greeting cards:
  artwork-decorated, 210
  dip-dyed, 194
Grow a Family Tree, 98-99
Guessing games:
  Botticelli Junior, 27-28
  Mystery Bags, 36
  Name That Number, 30
  You Don't Know What You're Talking About, 29
Guitar, rubber band, 174-75
Gummy Raindrops, 126

Haiku, 132
Hair accessories:
  Bow Barrette, 150
  Ponytail Holder, 148-49
  Ribbon-Covered Headband, 149

Hairy Harry, 71
Haunted hallway, 20-22
Have an Indoor Parade, 6-7
Headbands, ribbon-covered, 149
The Hidden Penny, 163
Hide-and-seek game, 66
Hide in Plain Sight, 37
Hobbies, picture books about, 130
How Many You's, 184
Huichol god's-eyes, 56

Ice Cream Sandwiches, 125
Ice-Cube Candles, 192
Ice cubes, lassoing, 82
Increase Your Allowance, 186
Indian god's-eyes, 56
Ink, invisible, 34
Interior design, 139-40
Interview Your Grandparents, 90-91
Invisible Ink, 34
Invitations, 17

J

The Jacks Tell All, 158
Jewelry:
    Dough Monster Chain, 146
    Friendship Bracelet, 42-43
    Magazine Beads, 147
    Safety Pin Bracelet, 151-52
Journals, 134-35
Junk Sculpture, 213

K

Kazoos, kooky, 169
Keep a Journal, 134-35
Keep It Dry, 165-66
Key chains, macramé, 45-47
Kitchen Garden, 74-75
Knot? Not!, 161
Kooky Kazoos, 169

L

Lanterns, silver, 190-91
Lasso an Ice Cube, 82
Lemon Drop Cookies, 120
Lima beans, growing, 74
Log Cabin, 204
Looms, making with straws, 54
Loopy Loops, 162-63
Lunch bags, personalized, 143

Macramé Key Chain, 45
Magazine Beads, 147
Magazine Scavenger Hunt, 39
A Magic Number, 181
Magic tricks, 153-66
    Banana Split, 164
    Chained!, 155
    Column by Column, 160
    George Flips!, 156
    The Hidden Penny, 163
    The Jacks Tell All, 158
    Keep It Dry, 165-66

Knot? Not!, 161
Loopy Loops, 162-63
performing in show, 154
The Psychic, 159
Unpoppable Balloon, 166
Vanna Vanishes, 157
Magnets:
    electromagnetic, 73
    for refrigerator, 195
Make Your Own Board Game, 24-25
Maracas, 172
Marbleized Stationery, 202
Masks:
    with features from different faces, 212
    papier-mâché, 200-201
Math games:
    Birthday Math, 188
    Nim Skills, 31
Measurements, using body, 184
Memory trick, 187
Merry Maracas, 172-73
Miniature God's-Eye, 56-57
Miniature Golf, 60-61
Mixed Green Salad and Vinaigrette, 112
Möbius strips, 162
Money:
    magic tricks with, 155, 156, 163
    making bookmark with, 191
Money Pouch, 144-45
Moody Blue, 28
Mosaic Planters, 193

Muffins:
Chocolate Chip, 118-19
Popovers, 107
Music, sing-alongs and, 15
Musical instruments, home-
made, 167-76
Cymbals, 175
A Drum to Keep the Beat,
170-71
Glass Chimes, 168
Kooky Kazoos, 169
Merry Maracas, 172
Nailhead Xylophone, 176
Rubber Band Guitar, 174-75
Shaker Bells, 175
Tinkly Tambourine, 173
Mysteries, 33-40
Buried Treasure, 40
Good Vibes, 84
Hide in Plain Sight, 37
Invisible Ink, 34
Magazine Scavenger Hunt,
39
Mystery Bags, 36
Pass It Along, 38
Secret Code, 35
Mystery Bags, 36

Nailhead Xylophone, 176
Name That Number, 30
Napkin fans, 3
Newspapers, with family and
neighborhood news, 86-87
Nim Skills, 31

Notebooks, artwork- decorated,
210
Number One, 178
Numbers, tricks and games with,
177-88
Birthday Math, 188
Forever 37, 179
Four Evermore, 185
Game of 20, 185
Great Memory!, 187
How Many You's, 184
Increase Your Allowance, 186
A Magic Number, 181
Name That Number, 30
Number One, 178
The Sum of Them, 182
Take It to the Nines, 180
Toothpick Tally, 183

Obstacle Course, 65
Open a Restaurant, 2-3
Opposite mornings, 14-15
Orange Cream Pops, 115
Orange seeds, sprouting, 75
Ornaments, colorful clay, 198-99

Paintings:
brushless, 47
decorating objects with, 210-11
portfolio for, 196-97
studio for, 18-19
Palindromes, 179

Paper clips, magic trick with, 155
Paper path race, 67
Paper Roses, 53
Papier-Mâché Mask, 200-201
Parades, indoor, 6-7
Parsnips, growing, 74
Pass It Along, 38
Pass the orange race, 68
Peach pits, sprouting, 75
Pennies, shining, 79
Penny Bookmark, 191
Pen pals, 136-37
Periscope Up, 72
Personalized Lunch Bags, 143
Pets, picture books about, 130
Photographs:
Bow Tie Wall Hanging, 94-95
fabric-covered frames for, 96-
97
for family or neighborhood
newspaper, 87
illustrating picture books
with, 130-31
making cartoon strips with,
128
making family photo album
for, 100-102
Special Event Album, 92-93
Picture books, writing and illus-
trating, 130-31
Pipe cleaners, projects with:
Paper Roses, 53
Twined Yarn Basket, 50-51
Pizza, French Bread, 105
Placemats, artwork- decorated,
210

Plan a Carnival, 8-9
Planters, mosaic, 193
Plants:
    Edible Sprouts, 75
    Hairy Harry, 71
    Kitchen Garden, 74-75
    Tabletop Terrarium, 80
Playhouse, log cabin, 204
Poems, writing, 132
Ponytail Holder, 148-49
Popovers, 107
Pops, Orange Cream, 115
Portfolios, for drawings and
    paintings, 196-97
Posters, travel, 13
Posture walk race, 68
Potatoes, growing, 74-75
Pretending, in Pass It Along, 38
Produce a TV Show, 10-11
The Psychic, 159
"Psychic" friends, 84
Puppets, transforming unlost
    gloves into, 207
Put on a Puppet Show, 16-17
Puzzles, two-sided, 32

Quesadillas, 106
Question-and-answer games, 24-
    25
Races, indoor, 67-68
Railroad cars, making from
    cartons, 12-13
Rainwater Watching, 81-83
Read All About It!, 86-87

Recipes, 103-26
    Baked Apples, 113
    Banana Smoothie, 121
    Banana S'Mores, 124
    Bird Food, 79
    Chocolate Chip Muffins,
      118-19
    Chocolate Crunch Bars,
      122-23
    French Bread Pizza, 105
    Frozen Bananas, 116-17
    Fruit Kebabs, 114
    general instructions for, 104
    Gummy Raindrops, 126
    Homemade Soda, 109
    Ice Cream Sandwiches, 125
    Lemon Drop Cookies, 120
    Mixed Green Salad and
      Vinaigrette, 112
    Orange Cream Pops, 115
    Popovers, 107
    Quesadillas, 106
    Trail Mix, 117
    Tuna Faces, 108-9
    Yogurt Cheese, 110
    Zesty Toasted Cheese
      Sandwiches, 111
Recyclables, projects with, 203-
    13
    Découpage Tray, 205
    Junk Sculpture, 213
    Log Cabin, 204
    Recycled Crayons, 209
    Scavenger Mask, 212
    Stained-Glass Window, 208
    Streetscape, 206-7

Unlost Glove Puppet, 207
Refrigerator magnets, 195
Relatively Trivial, 89
Restaurant, at home, 2-3
Ribbon-Covered Headband, 149
Roses, paper, 53
Rubber Band Guitar, 174-75

Safety Pin Bracelet, 151-52
Salad, Mixed Green, and
    Vinaigrette, 112
Sandwiches:
    Quesadillas, 106
    Tuna Faces, 108-9
    Zesty Toasted Cheese, 111
Sardines (game), 66
Scary stories, haunted hallway
    for, 20-22
Scavenger hunt, in magazines, 39
Scavenger Mask, 212
Science projects, 69-84
    Bath Cents, 79
    Blow Your Stack, 70
    Capture Your Shadow, 76-77
    Dollar Bridge, 77
    Electromagnet, 73
    Feed the Birds, 78-79
    Good Vibes, 84
    Hairy Harry, 71
    Kitchen Garden, 74-75
    Lasso an Ice Cube, 82
    Periscope Up, 72
    Rainwater Watching, 81-83
    Tabletop Terrarium, 80

Sculpture, made from junk, 213
Secret Code, 35
Secrets, invisible ink for, 34
Seeds, sprouting, 71
Sets and scenery, for TV show, 10-11
Shadows, creating indoors, 76-77
Shaker Bells, 175
Ships, making from cartons, 12-13
Shoe box shuffle race, 68
Silhouettes, 76-77
Silver Lantern, 190-91
Sing-alongs, 15
Skee Ball, 66
S'Mores, Banana, 124
Snacks. *See* Desserts and snacks
Soda, Homemade, 109
Special Event Album, 92-93
Special T, 142
Spiderwebs, yarn, 58
Sports, indoor, 59-68
    Balloon Volleyball, 63
    Bowling, 62
    Cup Catch, 64
    A Day at the Races, 67-68
    Miniature Golf, 60-61
    Obstacle Course, 65
    Skee Ball, 66
    Wastebasket Ball, 64
Sprouts:
    edible, 75
    Hairy Harry, 71
    Kitchen Garden, 74-75
Stained-Glass Window, 208

Stationery, marbleized, 202
Stories:
    haunted hallway for, 20-22
    writing with group of people, 129
Straight Curves, 48-49
Streetscape, 206-7
String and yarn projects, 41-58
    Brushless Painting, 47
    Friendship Bracelet, 42-43
    Knot? Not!, 161
    Lasso an Ice Cube, 82
    Macramé Key Chain, 45-47
    Miniature God's-Eye, 56-57
    Straight Curves, 48-49
    String Balloon, 44
    Twined Yarn Basket, 50-51
    Yarn Belt, 54-55
    Yarn-Covered Vase, 52-53
    Yarn Spiderweb, 58
String Balloon, 44
The Sum of Them, 182
Sweet potatoes, growing, 74-75

T

Tabletop Terrarium, 80
Take a Cruise…or Ride the Rails, 12-13
Take a Trip to Mars…Back in History…, 138
Take It to the Nines, 180
Tambourines, 173
Television show, producing your own, 10-11
Tents, for indoor camping, 4-5

Terrariums, tabletop, 80
Theatricals:
    Produce a TV Show, 10-11
    Put on a Puppet Show, 16-17
Time travel, 138
Tinkly Tambourine, 173
Tissue paper race, 67
Tissue paper roses, 53
Toothpick Tally, 183
Trail Mix, 117
Travel:
    in ship or railroad car made from carton, 12-13
    through time, 138
Travel posters, 13
Trays, découpage, 205
Treasure hunt, 40
Trees:
    for living-room campsite, 5
    for walls of haunted hallway, 20-21
Tricks. *See* Magic tricks; Numbers, tricks and games with
Trivia game, 89
T-shirts, decorating, 142
Tuna Faces, 108-9
Twined Yarn Basket, 50-51
Two-Sided Puzzle, 32

U,V

Unlost Glove Puppet, 207
Unpoppable Balloon, 166
Vanna Vanishes, 157
Vases, yarn-covered, 52-53

Videotape, of day in the life of
    your family, 88
Vinaigrette, 112
Volcano, in plastic bottle, 70
Volleyball, indoor version of, 63

Wake Up to an Opposite
    Morning, 14-15
Wastebasket Ball, 64
Water, pulling dry tissue out of,
    165-66
Water faucets, leaking, 82
Water glasses, moving water
    between, 83
Water tension, 81-82
Wearable works of art, 141-52
    Bow Barrette, 150
    Dough Monster Chain, 146

Friendship Bracelet, 42-43
Magazine Beads, 147
Money Pouch, 144-45
Personalized Lunch Bags, 143
Ponytail Holder, 148-49
Ribbon-Covered Headband,
    149
Safety Pin Bracelet, 151-52
Special T, 142
Windows, stained-glass, 208
Word definition game, 29
Woven yarn belt, 54-55
Writing:
    cartoon strips, 128
    haiku and cinquain, 132
    in journal, 134-35
    to pen pal, 136-37
    picture books, 130-31
    stories with group of people,
        129

X,Y,Z

Xylophone, nailhead, 176
Yard sales, 8-9
Yarn Belt, 54-55
Yarn-Covered Vase, 52-53
Yarn projects. See String and
    yarn projects
Yarn Spiderweb, 58
Yogurt Cheese, 110
You Don't Know What You're
    Talking About, 29
Your Own Cartoon Strips,
    128
Your Own Portfolio, 196-97
Zesty Toasted Cheese
    Sandwiches, 111